JUST THE BASICS

BABY

Instructions Included

THE PARENTS' PRACTICAL GUIDE TO THEIR NEWBORN BABY

TONY BAKERINK, M.D.

JUST THE BASICS

BABY

First Paperback Edition

Cover Photo © iStock.com / ReeseImages
Book Editing & Design: Cara Stein / BookCompletion.com

Contents

Dedicated to my three inspirations:
Chrissy, Tristan, and Cierra

Introduction

"Sometimes the smallest things take up the most room in your heart."

—*A.A. Milne / Winnie the pooh*

W hy write a book about pediatric newborn care when there are so many great big ones out there already? Well, it's just that: lots of very informative, *big* books have already been written. We live in an age of information. Parents can use the internet to research everything from A to Z about their child, as well as every type, style, and color of baby bottle ever invented. The problem is, new parents have access to so much information and so many answers—many of which disagree with each other—that it's easy to become overwhelmed. As a new parent, you may easily be confused by all the different answers and advice you will receive from vast and varying resources.

Despite all the information at your fingertips, sometimes it's most comforting to talk to a pediatrician. That's why I've written this book: to give you a quick introduction to what you need to know about babies, straight from a pediatrician.

I've spent about 16 years as a practicing pediatrician, going in and out of exam rooms and answering countless questions by many a wary and worried parent. In that time, I've noticed that I tend to answer the same questions over and over. Most new parents have the same concerns, and their questions tend to center around things like, "Why does my baby do this?", "Is it normal for my baby to be doing this?", and "Am I doing this right?"

The goal of this book is to answer the most common questions that many new parents have. I want to give you the information you need in a simple, straightforward way, so you can get up to speed quickly.

Babies don't come with their own instruction manuals, and there's an overwhelming amount of information out there. With this book, I want to provide you with a basic guide to how newborns work and what is normal. After all, as a pediatrician, I get to see a wide array of babies. I have the experience and expertise to recognize what is normal and what might be cause for concern. With this in mind, I decided to sit down and write my own version of an "instruction manual"—not only for my patients' parents, but all parents alike.

This little manual covers the most important and common topics that I think parents should know about. My goal is to give you a practical, realistic understanding of how and why babies do what they do, what they are about, and what to expect from your baby.

This book is not meant to be a substitute for your pediatrician. For that matter, it's not even meant to be a substitute for a big reference book. No single book can contain all the answers, including this one. Always seek out your pediatrician when you have questions or need advice. No other resource is more valuable than an expert in babies.

Instead, I intend this book as a quick-start guide. I hope that, after reading this book, you will have gained practical, realistic, and informative insights into how your newborn baby "works" and how she will "train" you to take care of her. (**Note:** To make sure everyone is included, I alternate between male and female pronouns throughout the book.)

With this book, I want to give you a solid footing for the first baby steps of your joyous journey with your baby. My sincerest best wishes to you, and happy parenting.

Congratulations!

Your world has just been turned up-side down.

Now what?

(Turn the page)

Jumping In

There's a lot to say about babies. When I sat down to start writing and researching for this book, I quickly saw how easily the project could balloon out of control and produce yet another big reference book. That would serve no other purpose than to act as a sedative. Instead, I decided to skip discussions about how to put a diaper on a newborn (trust me, you will become a pro at this in no time flat), how to dress a baby, or how to lay out all the items properly before giving your baby a bath. These subjects are all covered thoroughly in the big reference books.

Instead, I want to jump right in and talk about one guiding principle: simplicity. I will refer to Mother Nature a fair amount when writing to you, because I believe we can learn a lot from our natural world. In nature, we often find that simplicity is the key.

Many aspects of life are like that, including babies. The more we complicate the process, the more we work against the natural grain of things. That's why my goal here is to try and keep this book as simple as possible.

That's right: it's **simple**. We often make parenting much more complicated than it needs to be. In fact, your baby will train you and teach you over time. Soon, you'll become an expert on the subject of your baby.

I'll let you in on something you may not know. Newborn babies come into the world already prepared with thousands of years' worth of instincts and reflexes to aid them in survival. Believe it or not, as a parent, you also have very strong instincts that will kick in when this little one comes into your world. These instincts will aid you in taking care of her as well. We are hardwired for the task at hand—we just have to boot up the system.

Now, *simple* doesn't necessarily mean *easy*. Just because your baby has survival mechanisms built in, that doesn't mean little Zoey will immediately sleep all night and never fuss or cry. I'm sure you already know (or you'll soon find out): Little Zoey has different plans. A baby's toolbox of survival instincts actually includes crying, fussing, feeding every two hours, and generally not sleeping on your schedule.

Also, no matter how many books you read, remember that your baby hasn't read any of them. Babies only know what Mother Nature has instilled in them.

That's the basic premise of this book. It's not to give you the secret to finding the hidden "mute" button on your baby to stop her from crying. Instead, my goal is to help you understand why your baby may be crying, or why she might be doing a multitude of other things that worry or concern you. I want to give you a sense of what's normal and usual for babies, and help you make some sense out of this demanding little being that you have been blessed to care for.

Part 1

HOW YOUR BABY MAY APPEAR AT BIRTH

The Beginning

As a pediatrician, my journey with you begins after you have delivered your new little bundle of joy. Up to this point, your obstetrician and his or her staff have taken care of you and your baby. They have given you guidance on when and where to go to Labor and Delivery, what to bring, and how best to prepare for the delivery. They are experts at this, but if you need more information, you can also go to one of those big resource books. It will provide you with all the details on how best to prepare.

I strongly recommend going on a tour of the hospital where you plan to deliver. Familiarize yourself with the location of Labor and Delivery, the post-partum area where you most likely

will stay after delivery, the newborn nursery, and the Neonatal
Intensive Care Unit (NICU) if your hospital has one. In addition
to that, I definitely recommend setting up a meet and greet with
the pediatrician you have selected.

The delivery room

For the purpose of this book, I'm going to skip over any discus-
sion of labor and go directly to the subject at hand: babies. As
soon as your newborn infant is delivered, there are a few basic
things that will happen. After the umbilical cord is clamped and
cut, your infant will be dried off and placed on a warming bed.
His nose and mouth will be suctioned to clear any fluids or mucous that may be in his airways, and he will be immediately as-
sessed as to his well-being.

During the first five minutes, he will be graded on his per-
formance—the first test of many to come in his life. All babies
are observed for their heart rate, breathing status, color, muscle
tone (floppy or strong), and their ability to respond to stimuli
(called reflex irritability). This grading system is called Apgar
scoring. All infants will get at least two of these scores. The first
score is given at one minute after birth; the other is done at five
minutes.

The scoring system allows for two points for each parameter
being observed. Since there are five areas being observed, the
highest score a newborn can receive is a 10. A score that high is
almost unheard of, though. Virtually all babies have blue hands
and feet when they come into the world (called acrocyanosis).
Because of the blue hands and feet, we automatically deduct one
point for color. This is normal and expected. Most babies receive
Apgar scores of eight or nine at one and five minutes.

It's important for you to know that the first minute Apgar
score really doesn't carry much weight. If a baby has a score
under eight, that doesn't necessarily mean that there's something significantly wrong. Very frequently, newborn infants need

assistance in the way of physical stimulation, suctioning, and / or supplemental oxygen to assist them once they come out of the womb. The majority of the time, they will respond to this assistance very rapidly, within the first minute or two.

The five-minute Apgar score carries more weight. If an infant still needs intervention at the five-minute mark, then he may need advanced neonatal care provided by the neonatal or nursery team. That may require that he be observed and treated in the newborn nursery or even the Neonatal Intensive Care Unit.

However, even the five-minute score is often not predictive of how well an infant will do over time. All infants are different, and there's some debate as to whether Apgar scoring may even be outdated or less valid than once thought. These scores really just provide waypoints for us in pediatrics.

Caveat: I want you to know that most babies do very well at birth. In this day and age of great advancements in neonatal medicine, ultrasound technology, and obstetrics, the delivery team generally has a good idea of what to expect. They can prepare for any pre-existing problem (such as prematurity) and be ready to intervene if needed. Even if something unexpected does come up, institutions that deliver a lot of infants are quite adept at dealing with the curve balls that these little buggers can often throw at us.

While your baby is still in the delivery room, he will also be weighed, have his length and head size measured, and have his temperature taken. He also should receive a Vitamin K injection in his thigh. Vitamin K is given to babies at the time of birth because our vitamin K levels are low when we're born. Vitamin K is a necessary vitamin that aids in blood clotting. The birth process can often be traumatic to newborn infants, and as a result, they may be more susceptible to bleeding. The vitamin K injection is necessary to help keep your baby safe—do not decline it.

Most newborns are also given erythromycin eye ointment

to prevent the transmission of gonorrhea or chlamydia (sexually transmitted diseases) into the eyes, when coming through the birth canal. In addition, the first Hepatitis B vaccine is usually given soon after birth, in the thigh opposite the vitamin K injection.

Once your baby has been born and is deemed to be stable, he will often be bathed by the nursery staff and cleared to stay in the room with you. Congratulations! Your little one has gotten off to a great start. This moment marks the beginning of the rest of your lives together. Now all you have to do is water him, and he will grow.

Getting ready to go home

Once you have Little Zoey in your arms, there are a few basic things that we as pediatricians require in order to send her home. First of all, if she was born naturally (vaginal birth), she will most likely stay for at least 24 hours (sometimes longer) before being discharged to go home. If she was born by Cesarean section, then she will often stay two to three days. If there are additional concerns such as low blood sugar or jaundice (see the section on jaundice), her discharge might be delayed beyond this point.

One common cause of delay is a type of bacteria called Group B Strep (GBS). The majority of obstetricians will screen expectant mothers for GBS, usually around 35 weeks of gestation. Most women who have GBS show no symptoms, but to a newborn infant it can pose a risk for infection. If a mother is positive for GBS and delivers vaginally, we will often watch the infant in the hospital for 48 hours.

During labor, the mother will often be treated with intravenous antibiotics in order to decrease the likelihood of transmission of bacteria to the newborn infant, but antibiotics can't guarantee that the infant won't become infected. Therefore, in these cases, infants are often observed for 48 hours after birth. This will be up to your pediatrician. Sometimes, depending on the circumstances, a newborn may need blood tests to monitor for the possibility of infection. If you test GBS positive and have concerns, ask your obstetrician and/or your pediatrician how they will approach the care of you and your newborn in the hospital.

Beyond the typical length of hospital stay, an infant must also demonstrate several characteristics before being discharged from the hospital. To be allowed to go home, she must eat well (see the section on feeding), poop, pee, hold her own stable temperature, and show no physical findings that could pose a risk to her. Once she meets these additional criteria, she'll be allowed to go home.

Before leaving the hospital, many doctors (myself included) also recommend a hearing screening. Don't assume that your pediatrician will have the equipment to test a newborn's hearing in the office—it's specialized equipment that not all pediatricians have available.

After discharge, I often have my babies come to the office for a follow-up visit within two to three days. At this visit, we make sure the baby is feeding well, check that she hasn't lost too much weight, make sure she is not becoming more jaundiced (yellow), and address any questions and concerns that a parent might have. (Hopefully, this book will answer a lot of these questions up front for you.)

Going Home

It's time to go home! There's no going back now. That's right, there are no returns or refund policies on babies, so you can't trade Little Zoey in on a quieter model. She is your little creation who will go out into the world to make her mark. Since she didn't come with a set of instructions, let's talk about what to do next.

Car Seat

You must have a car seat before you will be able to take your baby home from the hospital, so I recommend that you get one in advance.

There are many different options for car seats. Find one you like that is within your budget and has a good safety rating. (You can often find safety rating information from consumer websites and magazines). Different car seats have a variety of different bells and whistles but, in the end, they all have to meet the same safety standards. You don't have to worry about getting the fanciest one.

Before it's time to take your baby home from the hospital, make sure you know how to fit your car seat properly. The hospital where you deliver may have personnel who are specifically trained and certified to install your infant's car seat properly. If you're not sure how to install it, check into this.

A few items for home

Besides the necessary items such as clothes, a safe warm place for your baby to sleep, formula and bottles (if you are not breast feeding), and stacks upon stacks of diapers, here's a short list of items that I think a new parent should have readily available. This list is not all-inclusive, and your pediatrician may make additional recommendations.

- Rectal digital thermometer
- Saline drops
- Bulb syringe
- Diaper cream/ointment
- Acetaminophen (Children's Tylenol)

You don't need a lot of fancy stuff—just the basics.

First, get a good **rectal digital thermometer.** There are many other types of thermometers for checking temperatures in infants, but a rectal temperature is the most accurate for a newborn infant. There are safety thermometers out there for taking rectal temps, and I would recommend them.

When taking the temperature, follow the operational instructions that come with your thermometer on how to "zero" it and read it, then use Vaseline or K-Y jelly on the thermometer tip and insert it no more than half an inch into the baby's rectum.

You don't need to check the temperature of your infant routinely, but if you feel that she might be ill or is behaving in any way that concerns you, getting an accurate temperature is very important.

Another important item to get is **saline drops.** These drops are used to keep your baby's nose clear. There are many different store brands, and you should be able to find them readily. They are all basically buffered salt water drops, and they all serve the same function: to aid in the removal of mucous from your infant's nose. Your infant is an obligate nose breather, meaning that he breathes mostly through his nose. He will not be able to eat or sleep well if he has mucous in his nose, so it's important to have these drops on hand.

In conjunction with the saline drops, you'll also need to get a **bulb syringe.** This tool is used to suction mucous from your infant's nose, when it is readily apparent. Take note, however, that overuse of the syringe for suctioning can cause trauma or bleeding, so don't use it excessively.

A good bulb syringe is worth its weight in gold. Usually, the hospital will provide you with one of these when the baby is born. I have found that the syringes from the hospital are usually the best, but they can be hard to obtain once you leave the hospital. Hold on to the syringe from the hospital when you get it—it will be invaluable to you.

Diaper creams or ointments are a must-have. Since babies poop and pee a lot, they tend to get sore red bottoms frequently. I would recommend having a good thick diaper cream (usually one with zinc oxide) to seal and protect your baby's bottom. Ointments are fine as well, and you will gauge over time what seems to work best for you. There is no one cream or ointment that is the best; it's all trial and error.

Acetaminophen is also something that I would have available in case your infant develops a fever after the first month of life. In the first month of life, any fever is a cause for concern, so if you detect a fever in your newborn, contact your Pediatrician straight away. But once your infant is past the first month of life, it's good to have acetaminophen on hand in case a fever pops up. It seems like fevers usually occur in the middle of the night. By already having acetaminophen on hand, you won't have to make a midnight run while your baby is sick.

Acetaminophen is also good to have on hand if your baby has had a circumcision (yes, it's ok to use Tylenol under one month of age for reasons of circumcision pain) and for later on, when he starts teething. Before giving Acetaminophen to your infant for fever or fussiness, I would recommend contacting your pediatrician's office to discuss the proper dosing and whether your infant actually requires the medication. We don't give Ibuprofen (Motrin or Advil) to infants under six months of age, so be sure to purchase Acetaminophen for your newborn.

What to watch for and when to be concerned

Most new parents worry about their newborns. That's natural when you don't have a good feel for what's normal and what might indicate a problem. Here's a short list of signs and symptoms to look out for. This list is by no means all-inclusive, but it covers the most common symptoms that concern us as pediatricians. If your infant exhibits any of these signs or symptoms, please contact your pediatrician or take your infant to the nearest emergency room equipped to take care of infants and children.

1. **Fever of 100.4 F (38 C) or greater** within the first month of life, taken rectally.
2. **Temperature below 97.0 F (36 C)** in any newborn, taken rectally.
3. **Poor feeding,** meaning you can't get your infant to feed despite repeated attempts to do so (whether breast fed or bottle fed).
4. **Large forceful vomiting,** especially if the vomit is green in color and/or associated with a distended (large and tight) tummy.
5. **Excessive sleeping or lethargy** associated with difficulty arousing your infant. You can try arousal methods such as removing clothes, opening up the diaper, flicking the bottom of the feet, or rubbing the back vigor-

ously. If your baby won't awaken, stir, cry, and otherwise act vigorous for you when you do these things, he needs to be evaluated.

6. **Inconsolable crying,** meaning that no matter what methods you are using to calm your newborn, she is continuously crying intensely and will not stop. This is also known as irritability. If you cannot calm your baby despite everything you have tried, she needs to be evaluated.

7. **Cyanosis (blue baby),** especially while feeding or accompanied by distress. In newborn infants, it is common for their hands, feet and around their mouth to have a bluish color to them, especially if they get cold. However, if your infant turns blue while feeding or looks like she is in any kind of distress with a blue color to her body, she needs to be seen immediately.

8. **Respiratory distress,** shown by sustained rapid breathing (brief rapid breathing episodes are normal). Also, if you see that your baby is pulling in her chest deeply when she breathes, pulling in between the ribs (called retracting), making grunting sounds, or flaring her nostrils, those can be signs of respiratory distress. Babies with respiratory distress may or may not also have coughing or look unusually blue. If you notice any of these signs, have her seen immediately.

9. **Any time you feel that there is something wrong** with your baby, please do not hesitate to contact your pediatrician. I have learned to respect maternal and paternal instincts throughout the years. These instincts are powerful, so when in doubt, call or have your baby seen by a pediatrician.

Why is my Baby Turning Yellow?

J aundice is the term that we use in medicine to describe the yellowing appearance of a newborn baby's skin within the first few days of an infant's life. Although not all babies get jaundice, about 60% of full-term infants develop some degree of jaundice.

There are two categories of jaundice. The first is what we call "physiologic" jaundice, which is not harmful to an infant. The second is what we call "pathologic" jaundice. This type can be the result of problems that may arise with a newborn infant. Pathologic jaundice may require medical intervention to make sure your baby is safe.

What causes jaundice, and why is it so common in babies? Jaundice is caused by a substance called "bilirubin," which builds up in your baby's bloodstream because the enzymes necessary to break it down have not quite kicked in yet in the baby's liver. As a result of this pigment building up in the bloodstream, your infant may start showing signs of jaundice (turning yellow).

With jaundice, the yellowing usually starts on the head and face first, and then proceeds down the body. Parents will often notice the yellowing in the eyes first, because yellowing is more noticeable and easier to see in the white background of the eyes than in other parts of the body. I also look at the tip of a baby's nose and his upper chest to help me assess how yellow he may be getting.

As I mentioned, physiologic jaundice is not harmful to your infant. This type of jaundice will usually resolve by one to two weeks of age, sometimes a little longer for breast-fed infants. If you think your infant is becoming more yellow over this time period, have your pediatrician evaluate him.

The second type of jaundice, having to do with certain disease processes that could potentially be harmful to your infant, is a very extensive subject that far exceeds the scope of this book. I say this, not to scare you, but so you'll know what to look for. That way, if there are signs that indicate possible problems with your baby, you can spot them early and get immediate attention.

Again, I want to emphasize that jaundice is very common. In the world of pediatrics, we see it virtually every day. Most hospitals in the U.S. have protocols in place to screen infants before sending them home, to help determine which ones will run a higher risk of becoming significantly jaundiced. If need be, we can intervene early, even before your baby goes home.

If your hospital or nursery doesn't screen for jaundice, see if you can request this prior to being discharged. It can be useful in predicting whether your infant may go on to have increased bilirubin levels that may require close follow up or additional intervention. Here are some of the risk factors for increased jaundice we use when screening infants.

Risk factors for increased bilirubin levels

- Elevated bilirubin level prior to leaving the hospital (the

first 24-48 hours)
- Premature delivery
- Family history of a sibling who had elevated bilirubin levels or required treatment for jaundice
- Infants with bruising from delivery or a collection of blood under the scalp (cephalohematoma) from delivery
- Infants who are strictly breastfed and experience a feeding problem or a delay in the mother's milk coming in
- Jaundice presenting relatively rapidly within the first 24 hours

To head off potential problems associated with jaundice, the most important factor is simply to have your baby checked by your pediatrician within two to three days of discharge from the hospital. At this visit, your pediatrician can give you further guidance and assistance for the jaundice if need be.

How do we treat jaundice? Most of the time, the treatment is relatively simple. For most infants, as long as we have checked a baseline level and the infant does not appear to be getting more yellow, we simply watch them and make sure that they are getting plenty of breast milk or formula so that they stay hydrated. The jaundice usually resolves itself before two weeks of age. If it lasts longer than that, you might want to contact your pediatrician.

A helpful little trick that you can try at home, to help the jaundice resolve sooner, is to do "sunbaths" with your baby. This is accomplished by removing the infant's clothes down to a diaper only. I usually tell parents to have the house temperature between 74 and 78 degrees Fahrenheit. You then place the infant next to a window INSIDE the house, WITHOUT the direct sunlight on him.

I usually tell parents to do three daily sunbaths, leaving the infant next to the window for about 30 minutes each time. Sunbaths usually only need to be done for a few days, hence the "rule of threes": 30 minutes, three times daily, for three days.

Even if it is overcast outside, you can still sunbathe your baby.

How and why does this help with jaundice? The spectrum of sunlight includes a blue wavelength of light that helps to break down the yellow pigment into a form that is easier for babies to excrete when they pee and poop. When this process is working, your baby's pees and poops will become yellow in color.

If you feel that your baby is getting worse, looks more jaundiced, or is simply not improving, have your pediatrician evaluate your baby. Some newborns need to have their levels of bilirubin (the substance that causes jaundice) checked again after leaving the hospital. If this happens with your baby and the level is found to be moderately elevated, your pediatrician may want to place your baby on home phototherapy. This is done with a special blanket that lights up blue. You can place your infant on the blanket to help the bilirubin level come down.

If your baby's level of bilirubin is quite elevated, he may need more extensive phototherapy in the hospital. If this happens right after birth, it could delay the baby's discharge to go home. If the baby has already been discharged, he may need to be readmitted to the hospital for phototherapy and possibly further treatment as well.

Either way, it's very rare for jaundice to reoccur once it's fully treated. You'll soon be able to close this little chapter in your infant's life and get down to the task of raising your baby.

What's Common in Newborns

I t's important for you to know that there is a range of normal characteristics in newborn babies. Some babies come into the world looking picture-perfect, whereas others resemble little aliens at birth. If your baby doesn't look quite how you envisioned right at birth, don't worry. Soon after, she will be as beautiful as you dreamed she would be.

Due to the limited space of the womb, as well as the effects of labor and delivery on her, your baby may have a wrinkled forehead, a flat nose, and even folded-over ears. All of these appearances are normal. Her head may also be a bit misshapen, and her eyes may be a bit swollen. She will have a "cheesy" substance all over her body called vernix, and she may have hair on her back, shoulders, and ears.

Although all of this may sound anything but attractive, these findings are normal and temporary. So you know what to expect, here are some common findings you may see in your newborn.

Head molding: This refers to the fact that all the bones of the baby's skull can overlay or slide past one another. The bones of the skull do this to allow the baby's head to mold to the birth canal for easier passage. This is why many newborn infants have somewhat cone-shaped heads.

These overriding bones can often be seen and felt as ridges on the scalp. They are normal. Over the first few weeks of your newborn's life, as his head starts growing, this issue will resolve itself.

The "soft spot": Many people have heard that babies' heads have a soft spot. What most people don't know is that there are actually two soft spots in newborn infants' heads. The main soft spot is also called the anterior fontanel. This is the larger one at the top of your baby's head. There is also a smaller one located at the back of the head, called the posterior fontanel.

You may have heard that you shouldn't touch your baby's soft spot because it might cause harm to your infant. Generally, this is not something you need to worry about. Although the soft spot feels open, it's actually covered by a thick fibrous sheet that is quite strong and protective. As a pediatrician, feeling the fontanel is the very first thing I do when examining an infant.

If you look closely at your baby's soft spot, you may see it pulse up and down with your baby's heartbeat. Some people will also tell you that you can check whether a baby is dehydrated by feeling the soft spot, but I don't recommend that. Feeling soft spots is not terribly accurate, especially for laypeople. If you're concerned that your infant may be dehydrated or that the soft spot is sunken, too big, or bulging outward, the best thing to do is ask your pediatrician.

Caput: This is swelling, usually at the crown (top) of the head. It's caused by fluid being pushed into the scalp during labor. Once your infant is born, the fluid usually absorbs soon thereafter, and the swelling resolves. Until then, the swelling is neither painful nor harmful.

Cephalo-hematoma: This is a collection of blood under the

scalp that occurs from the baby's skull bones rubbing against Mom's pelvic bones in the birth canal during labor. Sometimes, it can also result from the use of a vacuum assist device during delivery.

This blood collection feels like a little bag of fluid, and it is often found on the side of the skull. The cephalo-hematoma may get a bit bigger over the first few days but will usually resolve over one to two months as the blood is absorbed. Rarely, a hard "bony" knot may be felt months to years after, if the cephalo-hematoma "calcifies" (gets hard like bone). If that happens, it will get smaller as the baby's head grows. It will also soon be hidden by hair.

Scleral hemorrhages: Small collections of blood that can be seen in the white parts of the eye, caused by the pressure of labor popping tiny blood vessels in the eye. These are painless and usually resolve on their own within a few weeks. See the chapter on eyes for more information.

Scalp hair: Scalp hair is often dark at birth, and will start to shed after about a month. There are many possible shedding patterns: your baby may replace his hair gradually, all of it may fall out rapidly, or he might have a mixed pattern, such as the male pattern baldness look. There's no need to worry—this is normal.

Shedding is usually complete by about six months of age, and gradually your infant's mature hair will grow in. Your baby's final hair color may be totally different from that which is seen at birth. All bets are off on this one.

Body hair: This is only temporary hair, which is called lanugo. Lanugo is thin hair that can be found on the back, shoulders, and ears of newborn babies. This hair often rubs off by friction over the first couple of months (or at least hopefully before high school).

Umbilical hernia: This is a bulging out of the abdomen just above the belly button. This may not be readily apparent right at birth, but may become more prominent days to weeks later.

You will see it get bigger when your baby cries or strains to have a bowel movement.

It's important to know that umbilical hernias are relatively common. They are not painful, and they tend to resolve themselves from the inside, usually by two years of age. It's not necessary to treat this type of hernia or try to prevent it from getting bigger. You may have heard that you should place coins, Band-Aids, or belly bands over the hernia, but that's not necessary. In fact, none of these things work. If the hernia does not resolve by the time your baby is three to four years old, then it can be corrected easily with surgery.

Hydrocele: A hydrocele is a simple hernia that arises from a fluid-filled sac within the baby's scrotum. It may be seen on one side of the scrotum or on both sides. You can identify it by the fact that it's fluid-filled and can be compressed between your thumb and index finger. These hernias are painless, and they usually resolve themselves by one year of age. If not, they can be corrected easily with surgery.

On the other hand, if the area of your baby's groin swells during crying, this can be associated with a different type of hernia called an inguinal hernia. Hernias of this type need to be evaluated and possibly repaired much sooner than the other types. If you have any suspicion that your baby has a hernia, discuss it with your pediatrician.

Bowed legs: Most full-term babies have a natural "bow" to their legs. Parents ask me about this all the time. In most cases the bow is mild, and it's what we call a physiologic bow, meaning it's a normal part of the newborn baby's anatomy.

Due to limited space in the womb, babies like to keep their little legs and arms flexed up close to their bodies. Bowing of the legs facilitates this curled-up position and decreases the length of the baby within the confines of the womb. This natural bow usually corrects itself by six to 12 months of age.

In-turned, up-turned, or out-turned feet: Since there is limited space within the womb and infants are very pliable, they may appear to have one or both feet bent outwards, inwards or upwards at birth. This is usually due to positioning while the baby is in utero. As long as the feet can easily bend in all directions and are not rigid or stuck in any one position, these findings are normal and nothing to worry about.

Breech infants: The standard position for babies at birth is to be oriented with their head down toward the birth canal. When we say that an infant is born in the breech position, that means that the baby's feet or bottom is oriented down toward the birth canal instead. (Picture your baby kind of standing in the womb or being in a sitting position.) Although this orientation is right-side up for us when we walk around, it's upside-down for birth.

That may not sound likely to cause any problems, but it can result in the baby's hips not growing into their sockets properly. Ultimately, breech positioning may cause the baby to be born with something called hip dysplasia, where one or both hips may be out of socket. This is rare, but it is a possibility.

Thankfully, we are trained to look for this, not only in breech babies, but in all newborns. As part of the newborn physical exam and each subsequent exam (usually through six months of age), your pediatrician will do a certain hip maneuver to check for looseness or any signs that the baby's hips can be dislocated.

Regardless of the absence of physical exam findings, if your baby is born a breech infant, he should have an ultrasound at three to four weeks of age to assess for hip dysplasia. If your provider finds abnormalities on a physical exam or ultrasound, your infant will most likely be referred to an orthopedic specialist for evaluation and treatment.

If diagnosed early (ideally within the first two months), the treatment is usually pretty simple. It consists of placing your infant's legs in something called a Pavlik harness, which holds the legs in the correct position and helps them to grow into their sockets properly. With early diagnosis and treatment, most infants do very well and have no significant long-term effects from hip dysplasia.

Part 2

HOW YOUR BABY WORKS

Baby's Two Tools for Survival

Now that we've talked a little bit about how your baby may present at birth, let's move on to how your baby works—how and why he does some of the things he does.

Did you know that every baby needs two main tools to help him survive when he comes into the world? The first tool is that babies need to cry, and the second is that they need to suck. You may not view these two behaviors as tools (especially the crying), but they are both required for an infant to thrive outside the womb.

A newborn infant needs to be able to suck in order to eat. When they suck, they swallow food and therefore can gain weight and grow. Since a baby's food is liquid, sucking is the key. This may sound obvious, but it's really cool how babies come into the world already knowing how to do this. They don't get confused by trying to chew. Instead, they instinctively know how to suck.

Babies are feeding machines—their job is to act as if they are hollow and you can't fill them up. They're born knowing that they must eat and grow rapidly. This assures that a baby will thrive. This survival mechanism is built in because, once upon a time, only the babies that thrived were able to survive.

Similarly, crying is just as important as sucking. When Little Joey cries, it will have a powerful instinctual effect on you. It will make you go to him, because you will feel a *need* to fix the cry. This behavior will draw you to him to care for him. Ultimately, it will assist you in bonding with your baby.

I have often wondered why Mother Nature picked crying as a tool to draw us to our newborns, since it often feels so stressful and may even make us want to run in the other direction. Why not choose something more pleasant? But she knows much better than I. It certainly does work; I can't argue with that.

To illustrate the power of crying and how it affects each one of us, I often use the following example. What would happen if you put a sleeping baby in the corner of a room full of people? The people would wander by and look at how cute the baby was, and everything would be peaceful and calm. We all know instinctively not to wake the baby or he will cry.

But what happens when the baby wakes and starts crying? Well, as you can probably guess, a few things will happen. At first, people look at each other and maybe say, "Oh, poor baby." But if the baby keeps crying, it will start having an effect on everyone in the room. If he continues to cry, people will start asking where the mom is and why she isn't going to the baby.

Some people might gravitate toward the baby because they are drawn to fix the crying. Others might start pulling away or leave the room altogether. But ultimately, someone will pick up the baby and try to stop the crying. Until that happens, the baby's crying will affect every person in the room, in some way or fashion.

These instincts are very powerful. It's quite unnatural for people to leave a newborn infant crying and not intervene or pick him up. Our little ones are training us to bond with them. Pretty cool, huh?

Now, think about what would happen if babies didn't use crying as a tool for bonding and survivability. We would go about our day, getting our tasks done, and Little Joey would just hang out in his bassinet. If he never placed any demands on us, we would probably spend a lot less time with him. Because his crying and fussing prompt us to pick him up, nurture him, change him, and feed him, we interact with him often and bond with him.

When that's missing, society sees it as neglect. In nature, it's much worse: if you don't bond with your offspring, it dramatically reduces their likelihood for survival.

Now, I don't mean to imply that if Joey is not crying continuously, or if you aren't constantly picking him up and checking on him, that you will not bond with your baby. I'm just explaining why your baby comes into the world and behaves the way he does. His instincts and reflexes—as well as yours—are hardwired. So as long as you attend your infant and meet his many demands, you will do just fine.

Why does my baby cry when put down?

To get a little more specific about crying, one common question I get from parents is, "Why does my baby cry when I put her down, change her diaper, or remove her clothes?"

This is a matter of survival skills. Infants know instinctively that if they are put down in an open area (even a crib or bassinet) or laid out on a changing table, they are exposed and therefore vulnerable. By crying, they're sending you a message that says, "Wait a minute, I'm not supposed to be down here. I need to be picked up and held close, because that would be a safer place for me."

Babies know your smell. Your heartbeat soothes them, and

the warmth of your skin comforts them. This is why, in a lot of cultures, you see infants swaddled and carried right at the mother's bosom. They feel secure there because, instinctively, it's where they know they should be.

In newborns, it may seem that you can never put your baby down. It may feel like they're very demanding and a lot of work, with their constant sucking and crying. But remember, these are reflexes for survival. In full-term infants, these instincts will be quite heightened at first, but they will slowly start to dull over the next few months as you and your baby get more in sync with one another and learn to pick up on each other's cues. Your baby will acquire other means by which she will be able to get her needs met. The crying will become less, and the feeding and sleeping will become more regular. In time, you'll move out of the newborn phase and eventually into the later stages of infancy.

A brief word on crying

Remember that crying is a survival tool that is built into your baby so that you will go to him and attend to him. As a baby matures, bonds, and gains more skills and ways to interact with his world, the crying will become less frequent. However, when your newborn infant cries, you should go to him. You cannot spoil a baby at this age. There's no need to worry that you might be teaching him bad habits by being too attentive—habits form much more readily after six months of age. While he's a newborn, it's best to attend to his needs whenever he demands, and not just let him cry. Attending him is what ensures bonding.

When he cries, check the basics. Make sure he's not hungry, in need of a change, cold, or in pain. Make sure he shows no signs of becoming ill, such as having a fever.

If you've checked all of these things and he's still crying, then it's ok to let him cry for a little while. A little crying may help him to tire, ultimately allowing him to go to sleep. Or, you can try some of the tricks below.

Tricks to console your newborn

- You may try to calm a fussy infant by placing him on your chest, skin to skin. Infants find this comforting because they can feel your warmth, hear the calming sound of your heartbeat, smell your familiar scent, and sense the safety of being close to you.
- You may try swaddling him, walking him, or rocking him.
- Sometimes a ride in the stroller or car will do the trick.
- You could play soft music or rhythmic sounds for him.
- A warm bath may be helpful.

Your pediatrician may have some other recommendations as well.

Caveat: A fussy infant who cries for brief periods is not the same as a baby who is inconsolable. Inconsolability means that your baby cries much more intensely, and non-stop, despite all of your efforts to calm him. This pattern is much more concerning, and it needs to be brought to the attention of your pediatrician.

At a time like this, check his temperature and go over him from head to toe. Check for swelling or redness of an eye, where he may have scratched a cornea. Look for any signs of bruising, swelling, or redness on his body. Check the fingers and toes to make sure there isn't a hair wrapped around a digit, cutting into the baby's skin. If you still can't find anything wrong and can't calm him, have him seen by a qualified medical professional.

Colic

Colic is indicated when you see that an infant cries intensely and inconsolably for about three hours on a daily basis. Infants are not born with colic. This intense crying pattern comes on with time, starting usually after three weeks of life and continuing until it gradually resolves between three to four months of age.

We don't know what causes colic, but we do know it's not gas. There is some evidence that colic may have to do with bonding and comfort issues with a baby.

There are two main crying patterns associated with colic. The first and most common is that the infant cries excessively every evening for a specified period of time, usually not more than three hours. Then the crying resolves, only to return again the next evening. The pattern repeats until it gradually phases out after several months.

The second pattern is not limited to the evening. With this pattern, the baby will have intense crying for a specific period that can occur at any one time of the day. This pattern is less common. Like the first pattern, it will also resolve with time.

As a pediatrician, I often see people apply the term "colic" to infants who are just fussing, grunting, or straining—normal baby behaviors that don't need treatment. In contrast, we as pediatricians use the diagnosis of colic as a last resort. This is because any infant who is crying intensely and inconsolably for prolonged periods should first be evaluated to make sure he doesn't have a good reason for crying. Only after determining that the infant does not have an underlying cause for crying will we give the diagnosis of colic. If your baby is crying excessively, you should have him evaluated by your pediatrician to assess whether it's colic or some potentially more serious problem.

The only universal cure for colic is time, but some treatments can help soothe the symptoms until the baby has a chance to outgrow it. This varies from individual to individual—you'll have to experiment and find what works best for your baby. Here are a few suggestions to try.

Tips for colic treatment:

- Swaddle your infant or place your infant skin to skin on your chest.
- Wrap your baby and place her in a reclining swing or

vibrating bassinet.
- Walk with her or take her for a ride in a stroller or a car.
- Try sounds such as white noise, the vacuum cleaner, the stereo turned up, or the sound of the washing machine to calm her. (Do not put your baby on top of the washing machine. She could vibrate right off of it, onto the floor.)
- Apply warm washcloths to her tummy (check that they are not too warm) or give her a bath.
- Try giving the baby an ounce of cooled chamomile or mint tea, to see if this might have a calming effect. (Never use any fresh plant from the garden for this, but only prepared teas that you would find in the store.)
- Consider trying an old treatment called Gripe Water, which may have a calming effect on colic. This can be readily found at most major stores and pharmacies.
- Give her a massage, especially around her tummy.

If you try these tips but still have trouble calming your infant, I recommend a trip to your pediatrician.

Other Normal Stuff that Your Baby Does

We've spent a good bit of time covering crying and sucking, because they're such predominant forces in your newborn's life in the beginning. But those aren't the only reflexes and behaviors newborns come with that can puzzle or concern new parents. Newborns also hiccup, sneeze, and cough, to name a few.

Hiccups

I'm not sure why we get hiccups, but they're normal and harmless. Babies hiccup a lot when they first enter the world. Over the first few months, the hiccups gradually taper off.

Hiccups tend to bother us more than they bother the baby. Since they're not harmful, there's no need to worry about them or try to make them go away. We don't need to intervene by giving the baby sugar water, holding her upside down, blowing in her face, or trying other traditional old-time "remedies." The hiccups will resolve themselves, either on their own or through small frequent suck-and-swallows when the baby eats.

Sneezing

Unlike hiccups, sneezing has a known purpose: to clear the baby's nose so he can breathe. Babies are obligate nose-breathers, which means that they predominately breathe through their noses except when crying. For this reason, a baby's nose must be free of mucous or he will not be able to eat or sleep properly.

Let me explain why the sneeze reflex is so important. When your baby is born, he immediately must know how to handle drinking liquids, because that's what he needs to do to thrive. However, he must also know how to breathe while drinking all of this liquid. If he were to get confused and try to breathe through his mouth while sucking and swallowing, he could suck liquid into his airways. So Mother Nature protects him by making him breathe through his nose.

Just like we do, babies make mucous (boogers). As you can imagine, if the baby's nasal passages aren't clear, he will have a hard time eating or sleeping. This is why Mother Nature has instilled a sneeze reflex in your baby. When your baby sneezes, he is clearing his nose so that he can breathe better. It's normal and healthy for babies to sneeze very frequently, especially as newborns.

Clearing Cough

You may also hear an occasional clearing cough from your baby. This cough is to clear out any residual saliva, mucous, or retained formula or breast milk that may gather in the back of his throat. He will clear the secretions by himself, either by giving you this infrequent cough and or by swallowing the secretions.

An occasional cough like this is normal. However, a heavy, persistent cough is not. If you're unsure or concerned about how your baby sounds, contact your pediatrician.

Nose congestion

Believe it or not, the subject of nasal congestion is one of the most common questions that I get from parents, and it's fundamental to how your baby works.

Here are a few of the most common questions parents ask me when they bring their newborn in to see me soon after birth:

- Doctor, why is my baby so congested?
- Do you think my baby has a cold?
- Why does my baby breathe so loudly?

Many people ask this, because babies are naturally noisy breathers. They often sound congested at birth because the passages in their noses are small, so the breathing sounds are amplified. I often use the example of blowing through a straw. If you blow through a straw, you don't really hear too much, but if you put a little something inside the straw and blow through it, it will create a whistle sound.

The same effect happens with nasal passages. When babies breathe through their noses, it's like breathing through two small straws. The membranes in babies' noses disrupt the even flow of air and create a congestion sound. Because of this, some congestion sounds are normal. You can expect your baby to sound loud, especially when they feed, which is hard work for them.

Feeding a baby is like putting him on a treadmill to exercise. The baby will sound louder because he is having to work harder while feeding. Therefore, the sounds coming through the nose will be louder.

To understand this, imagine if you were told to get on a treadmill and start walking, but you could only breathe through your nose. At first, it would be no problem, but as the speed of the treadmill increased and you had to start running, your nose breathing would get louder and louder. This is why babies often sound especially loud and congested when feeding or crying.

If your baby sounds a bit congested, notice whether he can still eat and sleep, and whether his general demeanor has changed. If these things seem fine and he's not overly fussy, then the congestion sounds are probably nothing to worry about. Just be on the lookout for signs of problems.

However, if your baby's nose gets too congested, he will have a hard time eating and sleeping. You might see that your baby keeps trying to breathe through his nose despite it being blocked. When that doesn't work, he defaults to fussing and crying. This is also a survival instinct. Not only is crying a way to draw your attention to the problem, it also allows him to breathe through his mouth instead of his nose. Crying allows him to get the air he needs; the problem is that he can't sleep or eat very well at the same time.

When this happens, you'll know that your baby's nose needs to be cleared. To clean a baby's nose, you'll want to use the saline drops that we talked about having on hand (see the list of items for home). You'll place about three drops of saline solution in your baby's nose, then wait about a minute for the saline to soften the mucous. Then, use your suction bulb to suction out the nostril. You'll do the same thing for the other nostril as well.

Now that you know what to do, I want to emphasize that you only need to do this when the baby has enough congestion to actually cause trouble: fussiness or difficulty eating or sleeping. Do not chase the congestion sound in infants—these sounds are normal. If there are no readily seen boogers and your baby is comfortable and feeding well, you don't have to do anything to fix the sound. If you suction your baby's nose excessively when it's not needed, you can irritate his nose, thus causing more congestion and maybe even bleeding. If he can sleep and eat well, he will be fine. I find that most babies outgrow this "congestion" sound by four to six months of age.

Caveat: Do not make saltwater at home and put it in your baby's nose. If you get the proportions wrong, it may irritate your baby's nose. Also, do not put plain water in your baby's nose. We are made of saltwater, not plain water. Regular water is an irritant to the nasal membranes and will not be tolerated well by your baby. The store-bought brands of saline solution are properly balanced and best suited for use in your baby's nose, so I recommend using them.

Why is my baby awake all night?

First off, newborn infants have no respect for sleep schedules. In the hospital right after birth, they will often sleep a fair amount and may not be too demanding yet—the birth process takes a lot out of them. I also personally think that babies lay low at first and don't cry so much in the hospital on purpose. It's all part of their master plan to make sure you take them home with you, instead of trying to trade them in for a quieter model. This is just my personal observation, though.

In any event, those peaceful days don't last long. Soon after birth, you may notice that Little Zoey tends to come alive at night. There's a good reason for this. Think of it from Little Zoey's standpoint. She has lived her entire life up to this point in darkness. All of a sudden, at birth, she is pushed out into the light. She has no concept of light, and it's jarring after being in the dark for so long. It's like living in a cave for nine months and then suddenly walking outside into the bright sunlight. She will need a little time to adjust.

To understand how that adjustment happens, first you need to know that we all have a gland called the pineal gland, which acts as a "third eye," so to speak. It's located in the center of our brains, and its purpose is to sense the sun and the moon, and use them to set our body rhythms (called circadian rhythms). This is how our sleep-wake cycle and all of our body clocks get set.

When we're babies, our rhythms tend to involve more sleep during the daytime. That's because babies can sense the light, and it's not what they're used to. They're more comfortable being awake at night. You will just have to go with this. Mother Nature has it all figured out.

Your baby will need to start setting her own body clock with the sun and the moon. It's important to let her do this. She'll have a more regulated schedule down the road. Meanwhile, don't try and trick her into sleeping during the night by making it as dark as possible during the day so that she is awake more. This does not do your baby any favors and makes it harder for her to set her natural body rhythms.

Remember the simplest rule of all: Mother Nature is smarter than we are. As long as you don't try too hard to fix things that are not broken, your baby will adjust and do just fine. Throw out all the books on scheduling your baby's sleep in the newborn stage. She'll write her own book.

Newborn reflexes

As I've mentioned before, your baby will come into the world already wired for survival. Mother Nature has built lots of reflexes into your baby to help him deal with this new world. These reflexes are fully active in full-term infants, but they may be absent or not yet well developed if your infant was born prematurely.

To understand reflexes, think about the alternative. What if your infant was suddenly born into this world and had to learn how to do everything— eating, pooping, breathing, bonding, getting his needs met—all without knowing how to do it? If they had to take time to figure all these things out and learn how to do everything, they would get into trouble very quickly. If this was how life worked, I doubt many of us would have made it.

Instead, infants are born with the reflexes of thousands and thousands of years of ancestors who came before. These reflexes are very important to your baby. They give her a head start: the tools she needs to survive and start getting her needs met as soon as she enters the world.

Did you know that, for the most part, newborn infants do not use their higher brain functions? They make heavy use of the brainstem part of the brain, relying mainly on their innate reflexes for survival. We tend to look at newborns as tiny, help-less beings, but their instincts give them many of the tools they need to handle their world when they come into it. Using these instincts, your baby can guide you and show you what she needs.

Remember, even though you may be a first-time parent, Mother Nature has been doing this for a long time. She has pro-grammed both you and your infant to ensure your infant's sur-vival. Your baby will often train you and take you down the right path. You just need to pay attention and learn to understand her signals and cues. To help you, I'll explain some of the reflexes that are built into newborns.

Newborns come with a lot of reflexes. Some of them are quite purposeful, while others are not as well understood. Some are just plain baffling to me.

In this section, I'll cover the most common reflexes that I think you need to understand. For more detailed information or in-depth explanations of the vast number of reflexes that infants are born with, I refer you to any of the big reference books out there to learn more.

1. **Sucking reflex:** As soon as the breast or bottle is put in her mouth, your infant sucks without thinking about it. This reflex enables your infant to feed as soon as she is born.

2. **Rooting reflex:** This reflex is stimulated by stroking the baby's cheek or corner of her mouth, causing her to turn towards the nipple. When it's time for a feed, this aids in her finding the nipple.

3. **Moro reflex:** This reflex is stimulated by a sudden posi-tion change in your baby's head, such as a perceived drop. It can also be stimulated by a loud noise or some-thing that suddenly startles her. She will extend her neck, throw her arms out and then bring them back in

towards her body. Usually, this behavior will also be accompanied by a loud cry.

4. **Palmar grasp:** If you stroke the palm of your baby's hand with your finger, you will notice that she curls her fingers around yours and grasps your finger.

5. **Plantar grasp:** If you stroke the sole of your infant's foot, she will flex her toes and curl them tightly.

6. **Stepping reflex:** This reflex is elicited by placing your hands under your infant's arms and supporting her in a standing position. If you touch the soles of her feet to a flat surface, she will take a step as if walking.

Remember, these are just a few of the reflexes your infant will demonstrate when she is first born. There are many more, and they are quite fascinating to read about.

Periodic breathing

Parents often ask me about their baby's breathing pattern, because it seems to be varied and different from ours.

As adults, we have a very predictable and boring breathing pattern. We breathe in and out in a fairly regular pattern, at a rate of about 16 to 20 breaths a minute on average. However, full-term newborn infants are different than we are. The part of their brain that regulates their breathing hasn't matured yet, so their breathing pattern is very irregular. Infants can breathe slowly or very quickly. They can breathe in a regular pattern like ours or suddenly take a deep breath in, making a loud inspiratory breathing sound. Infants can also breathe very shallowly or hold their breath for short periods (usually less than 10 seconds).

The reason their breathing pattern is called "periodic" is because their respiratory pattern can be broken down into these different "periods" of breathing behaviors, rather than the regular pattern that we have, as the breathing center of the brain matures throughout infancy.

It's important to stress that it's normal for an infant's breathing pattern to vary over short periods. However, if your infant exhibits sustained deep or rapid breathing that does not seem to be resolving, you should contact your pediatrician to make sure your baby is not becoming ill.

Eating, Pooping, and Gas Concerns

"Don't ever tell a mother of a newborn that her baby's smile is just gas."

—*Jill Woodhull*

Digestion is another area where many parents have concerns. Here are a few that I hear often:

- My baby's stomach gurgles after I feed him.
- My baby seems to be in pain after I feed him.
- She has diarrhea after I feed her.
- My baby grunts and strains and pushes after I feed her.
- My newborn is always so gassy, is this normal?

These patterns are common among infants, and the reason is that feeding stimulates a reflex called the gastro-colic reflex. This reflex activates the gastrointestinal (GI) tract (stomach and intestines) to move after feeding, thus propelling food and swallowed air through the GI tract towards the anus.

Again, this is Mother Nature's way of making sure your newborn can do the basics when he comes into the world. That includes being able to poop without having to think about it. Pooping and peeing are reflexes. If your infant had to learn how to do these things before he could have a bowel movement or pee, he would be in trouble very quickly. So Mother Nature helps him along by giving him reflexes to handle the process.

When you feed your baby, you stimulate the gastro-colic reflex, which makes the bowels move. As a result, you may hear your baby's stomach make gurgling sounds. Many parents hear this and think the baby's tummy sounds upset. You may also notice that the baby draws his legs up, strains, or fusses a bit with a feeding or soon after. All of these behaviors are common reactions to the reflex that is stimulated by feeding him.

This is a normal reflex and a normal response from your infant. Grunting, straining, and a little fussing after a feed is normal. However, if your infant seems to be in significant pain with intense fussing or crying around or after feeding, you should probably run this behavior past your pediatrician just for good measure.

Many parents are also concerned about their baby's stools. Since the gastro-colic reflex is pretty active at birth and your newborn eats only liquid, you often see very loose stools in newborn babies. To be specific, you feed them liquid, and therefore, they poop liquid.

When parents see liquid stools, they're often concerned that their newborn has diarrhea. Intuitively, when we see liquid stools, we usually think of diarrhea. However, this is usually not the case in newborn infants.

True diarrhea is a disease process that most commonly will cause weight loss. Although your baby may lose some weight right after birth—some weight loss (up to 10%) is common and expected soon after birth—this is not related to normal loose stools. If you keep your newborn follow-up appointments with your pediatrician, he or she will follow your baby's weight and make sure that your infant is not losing an inappropriate amount.

The liquid stool phase in early infancy will not last forever. Your infant's intestines will get "smarter" soon after birth and begin to concentrate stool, thus making it more formed. Some of the first signs of this may be the presence of stools that have a texture like small seeds, cottage cheese, or paste. They will appear dark, thick and tarry green (meconium stools) immediately after birth, soon change to liquid green (transitional stools), and ultimately should appear yellow in color.

Interestingly, although babies tend to have very loose stool right at birth, they will often swing the other direction by the time they're a month or two old. At this point, the reflex dulls, and infants poop far less frequently. Infants who are formula-fed may only poop once every three or four days. Breast-fed infants may go as long as a week without pooping!

This tends to freak parents out, but there's a good reason for it, and it comes down to the difference between big kids and infants. Infants grow 90 miles an hour faster than big kids. To ensure their survival, babies must gain weight more rapidly than they ever will again in their lives. Most babies will double their birth weight by the time that they are four months old. Since they must do this by drinking liquid, they must eat continuously. This is why you will find that your baby is very demanding when it comes to his feeds. He does this because he is smart.

As the baby eats, most of the liquid he consumes will be absorbed and used to fuel his growth, with very little waste left over. Since babies are not eating big chunks of food like hamburgers, pizza, and baba ghanoush, they don't need to go all the time.

As adults, when we eat big chunks of food, our body uses only what it needs. We pass the rest out as waste. Your newborn, on the other hand, is drinking liquid and absorbing most of it for rapid growth. As a result, he doesn't have much waste, so he doesn't need to go as often.

Now, if your baby still poops multiple times a day, that's ok, too. Either way, I usually see babies develop a more regular stool elimination pattern after one to two months of age.

I wanted you to know these things and understand what's normal, so that you won't be alarmed if these things happen with your baby. On the other hand, here are some signs that are cause for concern:

- significant pain
- blood or mucous in the stool
- Persistent distension of the tummy, either with or without heavy vomiting, especially if the vomit is green.
- large and very frequent watery stools that seem to be in excess of the amount of liquid that your infant is taking in

If you observe these things, or any time you're concerned about your baby's bowel routines, I recommend that you contact your pediatrician.

Another very common digestive concern that I field is on the topic of gas. Many parents ask me, "Why is my baby so gassy?"

The short answer to this question is that your baby is built to be gassy. All babies are experts at it.

I spend a lot of time on this subject in my office, because parents are often concerned that the baby is in pain when they see him passing gas or squirming around after feeding. In reality, it's not as painful as we might think it is. It's often more frustrating to an infant than painful.

Nevertheless, parents are often very focused on and concerned about the fact that their infant is so gassy. I often see that parents have changed the baby's formula multiple times or that they have bought all kinds of remedies to fix the gas. I believe it's better to understand why babies do things and how they work, rather than feeding parents' concerns and looking for solutions to "fix" something that isn't actually a problem, so I'm going to explain this to you.

Babies are a set up to be gassy, just by the nature of what they do every day: sucking and crying. Both activities cause an infant to swallow a lot of air, and that air has to go somewhere. It comes out in the form of passing gas or burping.

If we were to x-ray the tummy of an infant when he's first born (not routine; this is for example's sake), we generally wouldn't see much but a little air pocket in the tummy called the "gastric bubble." This is from swallowed air, usually from the initial crying an infant does at birth. However, if we were to take an x-ray of the baby's tummy two or three hours after birth, we would generally see that air had travelled most of the way through the baby's tummy and intestines, all the way down to the rectum (the baby's bottom).

This is a normal finding. After birth, the baby swallows air while crying and while sucking and swallowing to eat. Since newborns spend their whole lives sucking and crying—their two biggest survival tricks—they end up spending a tremendous amount of time swallowing air. This air quickly travels through the baby's digestive system and comes back out in the form of burping and passing gas.

Have you ever wondered why we burp newborn babies and infants, but not two-year-olds? (No? You've never asked yourself this question? It must be a pediatrician thing.)

If you think about it, we don't burp two-year-olds because they don't spend the majority of their lives sucking and swallowing air while eating, as they did in infancy. They are also much more adept at getting the gas out than a newborn is. (This is usually demonstrated at the most inconvenient and embarrassing times while out in public.) Two-year-olds also don't spend as much time crying as newborns do. Instead, they strategically plan their crying for the most opportune time, such as the cereal aisle at the grocery store.

In the case of infants, about 20% of the gas that your little one produces comes from swallowed food. The majority comes from swallowed air. In reality, once the baby is born and is being fed (whether formula or breast milk), he should produce a fair amount of gas. Now that you understand why and know that this is normal, you can save yourself from worrying about tummy gurgles or trying to get rid of the gas. There's no need to switch formulas or try to solve this "problem"—it's not a problem at all, it's normal.

Many parents also get overly concerned about burping their baby. I see parents who must get that burp out of their baby after each feed, no matter what, or they cannot rest easy.

Trust me, the air will come out of one end or the other all by itself. You don't need to do a lot to your baby to try to force it to happen. Certainly, burp your baby for a minute or so with each feed, but if you don't get a burp each and every time, don't worry about it.

Food is Good

Feeding a newborn infant is a huge subject that could easily take up a couple of chapters. But since our goal is to break it down and make it easier to digest (pun intended), I'll stick with the essentials. You can always consult a big reference book if you want to know more.

Breast feeding

Mother Nature pretty much has this part figured out for us. For thousands of years, breast feeding was the sole source of food for newborn humans. Besides the innumerable dietary benefits that aid in digestion, absorption, brain growth, and development, the natural components of breast milk have also allowed the human race to propel itself forward through the transmission of natural immunity from mother to baby, by the passage of protective antibodies. In short, breast milk is magic liquid made by humans for humans. It's very good stuff.

In deciding whether to breast feed, many parents want to consider the pros and cons, so I'll highlight those here.

The pros of breast feeding:

- It's cheaper than formula
- It decreases the number of infections that an infant may get (this varies depending on other factors)
- No preparation needed (no sterilizing bottles or mixing formula)
- It may help Mom get back into shape quicker, as breast feeding burns calories and helps the uterus contract down
- The constant skin-to-skin contact directly contributes to bonding while feeding

The cons of breast feeding:

- Honestly, if the feeds are going well, there are no maternal risk factors (certain infections or medications) and the mother has a good supply of milk, there really are none.

So, how does breast feeding work? You might expect that, as soon as your baby is born, you will put her to your breast and she will immediately start feeding. Mother Nature has had thousands of years to perfect this process, so it must be easy, right?

In reality, it's not always that simple, but the method is well established. It definitely helps to put the baby to the breast as soon as possible after birth, so as to start establishing the feeds and to initiate your milk coming in, but this is only the first step.

In the beginning, you have a bit of leeway to start the ball rolling. When your baby is born, she has a lot of water stored up in her little body. There is a reason for this. It takes about two to three days on average for the mother's milk to come in. During this time, when you are putting the baby to breast, she is only getting a small amount of colostrum (early milk) and not much else. That's normal.

It's important to remember that, when your baby is first born, she doesn't need much more than this small amount of fluid because she has that extra water on board. Meanwhile, by putting her to breast frequently, you will send the message to your brain that in turn will send the message for your milk to start coming in. Mother Nature has provided this time buffer for you and your baby to start getting in sync with one another.

During the first few days, if the baby is breast feeding well, there is not a lot of need to give your baby formula. Mothers often tell me that since their milk is not in immediately, they need to give their infant formula. I like to remind them that the baby has extra water. If he's latching well, he should also be getting some colostrum. For most babies, that's enough to meet his needs for the first few days.

Of course, there are exceptions. In some special cases, your hospital staff or pediatrician may recommend supplementing with formula. A good example of this is that some infants experience a drop in blood sugar soon after birth, for various reasons. If the infant is not getting enough sugar from the colostrum to keep the sugar level up, the baby may need some supplementation to be safe. The hospital staff and your pediatrician are well versed in the problems that can arise with breast feeding and the birth process, so they can make the best recommendations for your specific case.

When starting out with the feeds, it is generally recommended to put the baby to breast at least every two to three hours. This stimulates the milk to come in, and it matches a typical newborn feeding schedule.

Your baby may want to feed more frequently, or she may want to sleep a bit longer between feeds. At birth, as long as the baby doesn't want to go longer than four hours between feeds, I recommend feeding the baby as she "demands." I recommend following your baby's lead, rather than trying to schedule your baby right at birth, because your baby's instincts are to come into the world and eat continuously. She needs to do this in order to gain weight. It's a challenge to gain weight so quickly by drinking a thin liquid, so expect that she will demand to feed a lot.

Babies act as if they are hollow and you can't fill them up. That's all part of their survival instincts. If she demands, then you feed. Don't worry about feeding too much—if she over-feeds, she'll simply give it back to you. Then you'll know to cut back a little on the next feed.

Infants should be little feeding machines when they come into the world. I generally don't worry about the infant who is an avid little eater. It's the baby who likes to slumber more than eat that I tend to watch a bit more closely. Now, babies are smart, but they can also be a bit lazy at times. Some babies decide right off the bat when you put them to breast, "Hey, if I'm not getting much, why should I work for it?" These are the little buggers we have to work with a bit.

I mentioned earlier that newborn babies shouldn't go much longer than four hours between feeds. There's a reason for this. Our adult bodies have a lot of sugar (glucose) stored up in our livers. This sugar is constantly being released into our blood stream. We need this sugar to be available continuously in order for our brains to function properly.

When babies are born, they don't yet have these stores of sugar built up, so they need to feed frequently to maintain the sugar levels in their bodies. If your baby sleeps for prolonged periods, she may experience a drop in blood sugar. (This is rare, but it can happen). Also, since your baby needs to gain weight very quickly when she comes into the world, sleeping too long may cause her to miss out on feeding opportunities and not get all the calories she needs to grow.

That's why I usually recommend feeding your baby as she demands for the first months of her life, as long as it isn't longer than four hours between feeds. After the first month, your baby's glucose reserves will be built up in her liver and she should easily be able to sleep for longer periods, although I doubt she will. Most babies only want to sleep long periods when they shouldn't, and want to feed very frequently when you want them to sleep longer. It's a grand conspiracy, well thought out by all babies. I'm pretty sure they have secret meetings.

What can you do if your baby is a "sleeper baby" for the first month? Basically, you need to wake her up and get her to feed at least once every four hours. One way to do this is to undress the baby and open up the diaper. I'm not saying you should leave your baby exposed and out in the open in a cold room, but a few unclothed moments will often be enough to get your baby moving around and possibly even fussing at you. If this gets your baby going, attempt to feed her.

Sometimes, though, you basically have to make them mad before they will feed. I usually recommend lightly "flicking" the bottom of your baby's feet or taking her receiving blanket and rubbing her back fairly vigorously. Babies don't particularly like either of these things, and they may get a little upset. Once you've got them awake and a little mad, they'll usually give you a better and more aggressive feed.

There are many other tricks you can try as well. Basically, you're trying to get them to awaken and be little bit peeved so that they will feed better.

If you can't get your baby to feed while you're in the hospital, contact the nursing staff. They can work with you, and they'll contact your pediatrician if they feel that there is a problem.

The same is true after you get home. Your baby is supposed to be an avid feeding machine when she comes into the world. If you have any concerns about poor feeding with your infant, contact your pediatrician straight away. Don't wait until the next follow-up appointment.

Aside from infant laziness, there are a few other glitches that can come up with feeding. Even though Mother Nature has this wonderful process of feeding *almost* perfected, she hasn't quite worked out all the bugs as of yet. A few common difficulties with breast feeding include a poor latch, a painful latch, or problems with sucking and swallowing. The mother's nipples may also be too big, inverted (pointing in), or flat. And, of course, the mother may be very tired or in pain after delivery.

Difficulties like these may make the act of breast feeding a challenge in the beginning, but most infants are able to breast feed well with a bit of persistence and the right help. The key word here is "help." While you are in the hospital, if possible, have a lactation consultant come and meet with you. If the hospital does not have a lactation consultant, most nursery nurses are well-versed in the nuances of breast feeding and should be readily available to assist and guide you.

Most importantly, before you leave the hospital, your pediatrician should assess your comfort level and the baby's ability to properly feed, and discuss these things with you. Feeding is crucial, so if you're uncomfortable about the way the feeds are going, then if at all possible, stay in the hospital a bit longer until you are comfortable.

If a prolonged hospital stay is not possible, then ask for contact information for a lactation consultant and arrange for an outpatient assessment as soon as possible. I also recommend a follow-up appointment with your pediatrician two to three days after discharge from the hospital. I recommend this for all babies, whether breast fed or bottle fed, to make sure that any potential problems can be caught and addressed early.

A few finer points on breast feeding:

- You do not have to "toughen up" your nipples to prepare for breast feeding. Mother Nature will prepare your nipples for the task at hand.
- Breast feeding shouldn't be painful. If you experience significant pain while breast feeding, get some assistance by a trained professional.
- Get a good breast pump. I usually recommend the electric over the manual pumps. The hospital staff, your pediatrician, or your lactation consultant can make recommendations for you.

- Get the contact information for a good lactation consultant, because she will be an invaluable resource to you.
- Breast milk can be frozen for a month at a time in a standard freezer or three to six months in a deep freeze. Get good grade breast milk storage bags for this. Label them and date them, and use the oldest first.

Opinion: I think it's important to stress that, even though breast feeding your newborn is highly recommended, there are times when breast feeding simply doesn't work, despite all of your best efforts. There may be reasons that a mother cannot breast feed her newborn infant, or she may simply choose not to do so. In this day and age, when breast feeding is held in the highest regard, it's all too easy to make moms feel as if they are doing something horribly detrimental to their infants by giving them formula. I even had one Mother tell me that she would never give her baby that "poison" (formula). I thought to myself, "Well, let's certainly hope that all goes well then with your breastfeeding—otherwise, we're going to have to get quite inventive."

My point is that breast milk is good, but the infant can do just as well with formula. I know that some breast-feeding advocates will bristle at a statement like this, especially coming from a pediatrician. They will tout all the studies proving the wonderful benefits of breast milk, and I would not argue with them. There definitely are benefits to giving your baby breast milk, including increased immunity, decreased allergies to foods, and possibly even increased IQ. However, sometimes parents simply cannot breast feed their infant, or they choose not to. Then what? Do we imply that something will be wrong with their child?

From my perspective, if you can breast feed your baby and you want to do so, that is wonderful. As a pediatrician, I am going to use all available resources to make this happen to the best of your ability and the baby's. On the other hand, if you go the formula route for whatever reason, I am still going to use all available resources to ensure that your baby feeds and grows just as well. Until I see a study showing that all of the world's geniuses were solely breast fed and all under-achievers were formula fed, I will maintain that infants grow and thrive on both types of food sources. As a pediatrician, that is what makes me happy.

Formula

When it comes to formula feeding your newborn infant, confusion can often arise. Many parents have concerns as to which type of formula to use and how much to give the baby. There are many types to choose from, so it can be overwhelming. Here are some guidelines to help you, but remember that these are only guidelines. Your pediatrician will help you fine-tune the feeding based on your baby's growth parameters.

Before I discharge a baby from the hospital, he must be able to suck and swallow well. Healthy full-term babies should be able to take a minimum of one to two ounces on average, every two to three hours. Your baby should be able to do this with relative ease, usually in 20 minutes or less.

Over the next couple of weeks, he should gradually increase his intake to two to three ounces every two to three hours. If he wants more, feed him more.

It's a simple rule with babies: if you don't feed them enough, they will not grow, but if you give them a bit too much, they will just give it back to you. If that happens, you can adjust accordingly at the next feed.

Within the first month of life, most babies will feed about every two to three hours. If he wants to sleep up to four hours, he may. However, if he wants to go longer than this without a feed during the first month, I would wake him and feed him. Remember, newborn infants should be little feeding machines.

It is not uncommon for your baby to spit up a small amount

of the formula when he starts to feed. I see a lot of this in the hospital, especially when a baby is first born. This spitting up is often a cause of great concern for the parent, but usually it needn't be. It makes sense if you understand why it happens.

Immediately after a baby is born, one of the first things we do is feed him. The only problem is that, at that point, your baby's tummy has never seen food before. Before birth, your baby's stomach and intestines haven't really needed to do much work yet. As a matter of fact, they're kind of dormant. That's why babies don't normally poop while inside the womb. So, when the baby comes out, there is still a lot of swallowed amniotic fluid and mucous in the stomach. Since the stomach and intestines are just starting to wake up and figure out what to do, these liquids and secretions will often go in both directions, as will any food we give them.

Usually, the first sign of things moving in the right direction will be the passage of meconium. This is a thick, sticky, dark green substance that is composed of all the intestinal by-products (sloughed cells, mucous, bile) that have collected in your baby's intestines throughout his stay in the womb.

Soon after birth, you can expect your baby to start "decompressing" and getting this stored up tarry substance out of his intestines. When you start feeding your baby, you will stimulate the gastro-colic reflex (remember the reflex we talked about in the section on pooping?), which will start moving things in the right direction. But until then, you may see formula, mucous, and amniotic fluid come back up the wrong direction. This does not necessarily mean that your baby doesn't tolerate the formula and needs to be switched. In most cases, it's just that your baby's system needs time to wake up. However, if you feel that your infant is having a significant problem tolerating his formula, talk to the nursing staff and/or your pediatrician.

Caution: If your baby doesn't poop within the first 24 hours, this could be a cause for concern. Other warning signs include large vomits (as opposed to small, frequent spit-ups), green vomit, or a big, distended belly (like a drum). If you see any of these signs, notify your pediatrician immediately.

If feeding doesn't go smoothly right away, many parents become concerned that the baby is lactose intolerant, especially if other people in the family are lactose intolerant. Due to this concern, parents often want to switch the infant to a soy-based formula or a formula devoid of lactose.

In reality, true lactose intolerance usually comes on with age. It's rare to be born with none of the enzyme needed to break down lactose. Although Little Joey may become lactose intolerant down the road, this rarely happens at birth. I seldom recommend or see the need to switch the formula right after birth for this reason.

Many parents are also concerned that their baby is allergic to his formula right at birth. This, too, is very rare. Most often, if a newborn is going to be allergic to his formula, it will manifest a few weeks down the road with painless blood in the stools or atopic dermatitis (heavy patching of dry skin, usually over the majority of the baby's body). If either of these findings occurs, contact your pediatrician—a simple change to a hypo-allergenic formula may help to quell the problem.

Many parents are also concerned about the taste of the formula. They worry that their baby doesn't like the flavor. Although this could be the case, the reality is that babies' little taste buds are not well formed yet.

If you want to test this out, go get a bottle of formula and give it a taste. It doesn't matter which brand you try—any one of them will challenge your taste buds, because none of them taste particularly good to us. But think about this: your baby never seems to get tired of this liquid, which he will drink continuously for the entire first year of his life. Can you imagine eating the same food every day for a whole year and not getting tired of it? Your newborn can and will, so pick a regular formula and forge ahead.

Choosing a formula

Looking at the many different varieties of formula, it's easy to get overwhelmed. How do you know which one to choose?

One day, I decided to conduct an experiment. I was in the store with my two teenagers, so I dragged them over to the formula aisle and told them we were going to look at formulas. (They were thrilled.)

Now, these kids have virtually no knowledge of formulas, so I figured I would use them as my guinea pig control group. (They are still under age, so technically it's ok to use your children for experimentation with your own consent.) I asked them to find the formula that they thought would be best for a newborn baby. Then I stepped back and watched the experiment unfold.

First of all, here are some of the different types of formulas they had to contend with: "total comfort," "sensitive," "soy," "hypoallergenic," "spit up" (remember, most newborns spit up some), "organic," "nourish," "gentle," "soothe," "protect," "advantage," "tender," and "premium."

I watched them debate over whether they would recommend an "organic" formula because they thought it would be the healthiest, or a formula that implied it would "protect" the baby. Or, what about "advantage"? With a name like that, maybe the infant would have some kind of an edge over those babies who only got "soothing" or "gentle" formulas.

The debate continued as they wrestled with wanting to get the best formula. If they picked one such as "total comfort," but didn't pick the "organic" one, would the baby be losing out somehow?

In the end, my son just picked the biggest container because he felt it would be cheaper, and my daughter picked the "organic" because she is all about going green.

As my little experiment illustrates, there are a lot of choices available when it comes to formulas. It's not always easy to decide which one to choose. As a pediatrician, even I am sometimes confused by all the different choices of formulas offered. I took biochemistry once upon a time, and I don't recall ever learning about "softer" and "gentler" proteins. I'm not even sure what this means, but it's often marketed to both consumers and pediatricians alike.

It's confusing, and parents just want to do what's best for their infants. Here's a quick guide to help you understand the various types of formulas and the differences between them.

Cow's milk-based formulas: These formulas are the most commonly used and tolerated by infants. The main difference between regular cow's milk and a formula based on cow's milk is that the formulas are treated to make the proteins more digestible for your baby.

Most formulas are also supplemented with iron, which is necessary to help prevent anemia (low blood) in your infant. Never use low-iron formulas with babies. Some people believe that the additional iron in formula causes constipation, but that's a myth. There is not enough iron in formula to cause constipation.

Soy formulas: Instead of being made from cow's milk, some formulas are made from soy. In these formulas, the protein is different (soy instead of casein or whey found in cow's milk). The sugar is also different from the lactose found in cow's milk: usually glucose or sucrose.

I rarely recommend these formulas, because they serve little purpose in an infant's diet. If I believed an infant was allergic to cow's milk-based formula, I would not switch her to soy. There's a simple reason for this: a large percentage of babies who are allergic to cow's milk protein are also allergic to soy protein. In cases of allergies, I bypass soy formulas and go straight to hypoallergenic formulas (see below).

You may also have heard that soy formulas decrease colic and fussiness in newborn infants. There is no real evidence to support that claim.

Hydrolyzed formulas (hypoallergenic formulas): The proteins in these formulas have been treated in such a way as to make them easier to digest and less likely to cause allergic reactions. I use these formulas in infants who show signs that they may be allergic to their formula—symptoms such as painless blood in the stools or moderate eczema (dry, itchy skin).

Hydrolyzed formulas are more costly. If you're considering using this type of formula, I recommend discussing the idea with your pediatrician first.

Specialized formulas: These formulas are for specific medical disorders, and also for premature infants. You would start one of these formulas only at the direction of your pediatrician or another doctor.

How to Select a Formula for Your Baby

Now that you're familiar with the general types of formula available, you may still have a lot of questions about which one to pick. After all, I haven't mentioned anything about "organic" vs. "advantage" vs. "comfort."

My recommendation when starting a formula is simply to find a standard formula that has been on the market a long time and is economical. Despite the many marketing claims made about them, most standard formulas are basically the same. They all provide virtually the same nutrition. Humans are humans, and we all require common basics of nutrition. This applies to newborns as well. This is why the elements of most standard formulas are the same.

The differences from one formula to another represent slight changes related to their proteins and sugars. This is what allows one formula company to focus its marketing claims on "soft" proteins and "total comfort" as compared to another company's formula. The essentials of nutrition are what they are, and all of the formula companies update their recipes to keep pace with advances in nutrition. So take "comfort" in the fact that any standard formula will give your baby good nutrition—just as good as the next baby gets. There is no one formula or company that has the absolute best formula.

If all standard formulas are mostly the same, you may be wondering why there are so many formulas on the market. The reason is that the formula companies cater to parents' concerns regarding their babies, creating slight variations and packaging targeted to these concerns.

As parents, we all have an inherent need to do the best thing for our newborn infants. If you are not sure which formula to pick, ask the hospital staff or your pediatrician to make some recommendations while you're in the hospital.

Some additional points on formula feeding

- **Price:** Ready-to-feed formula is more expensive than concentrated formula. Powder is the least expensive.
- **Storage:** You can prepare formula in advance and leave it in the refrigerator for up to 24 hours. Warm it by running under warm water or by letting it sit at room temperature for an hour. Despite what it says on the formula label, you do not have to discard formula after it has sat out for only an hour. If you do that, you will end up throwing away a ton of formula, which does nothing more than support the formula companies. Formula can easily stay out for several hours at room temperature (not in the heat of the day) and still be safe for consumption by your newborn. Use common sense and good judgment here.
- **Cleaning and sterilizing bottles and nipples:** If your water contains chlorine (most city water supplies do), there is no need to sterilize the bottles or nipples. You

can either place them in the dishwasher or wash them with soap and hot water. If your water is not chlorinated, you should boil the bottles and nipples for five to 10 minutes prior to using them.

- **Choosing bottles:** When picking the types of bottles to use, there is no one bottle or nipple that is better than the other. I like any bottle that is aimed at decreasing the amount of swallowed air your infant receives while sucking. The bottles with plastic liners allow you to express the air out more readily, but they are a bit more expensive.

- **Choosing nipples:** There are special nipples designed for specific medical needs, but for most full-term newborn infants, I usually just recommend getting a regular nipple. You want a nipple that allows your infant to feed readily without having to work too hard, but does not allow too much liquid to flow at a time. If your infant has to work too hard to get the formula, he might get frustrated during feeds or simply shut down and not feed. On the other hand, if he gets too much liquid, he may let a lot of it run out the sides of his mouth, or he might get flooded and start coughing and sputtering. You want a happy medium.

- **Feeding position:** When feeding your baby from a bottle, always feed him in a reclining position. Do not feed him lying flat on his back, and never prop the bottle, as this increases the likelihood of both choking and ear infections.

- **Feeding water:** Do not give bottles of water to newborn babies. It doesn't matter whether they are bottle fed or breast fed.

There are two main reasons for not feeding babies water. First of all, your baby needs all the calories she can get when starting out, because she is growing faster at this age than she ever will again. If she is getting water in place of either breast milk or formula, she is missing out on much-needed food to fuel her rapid growth.

The other reason we don't give plain water to babies is because they can have a seizure if they get too much. This may sound crazy—most people think of water as very innocuous, and we spend so much time fighting with our older kids to drink more water. How could it be bad for babies?

However, newborn babies are different than we are. They're kind of like little bags of salt. Our bodies use salt to make our nervous systems function properly, and it must be kept in a fine balance. When we give too much water to a baby, it dilutes the salt. As a result, the baby's nervous system cannot work properly, potentially triggering a seizure in a newborn infant.

After four months of age, I will often loosen the restriction on water. At that point, parents may give four to six ounces of water per day if they would like. However, babies really don't need water. If you're concerned that your child might be thirsty, you can give him formula or breast milk. Both contain all of the water that a baby needs.

Vitamins and supplements

Breast-feeding mothers who eat a healthy and balanced diet and continue to take their prenatal vitamins generally pass adequate vitamins to their newborn, with a few exceptions that we will discuss below. Formula-fed infants generally receive adequate vitamins in their formula and do not usually need additional vitamins.

Vitamin D: Breast-fed infants need additional vitamin D, because very little is obtained through the breast milk. They need at least 400 IU daily. This can be obtained by giving your infant a daily over-the-counter supplement of vitamin D drops or by giving him daily multi-vitamin drops that contain the same amount of vitamin D.

Formula-fed infants will often get enough vitamin D in their formula.

Iron: Babies who are strictly breast fed receive sufficient iron from breast milk to prevent anemia (low blood) during the first six months of life. After that time, to prevent anemia, parents will start adding iron-fortified foods. These will help to bolster their infant's iron stores.

Infants who are formula-fed should always be on a formula with iron. There is no place for low-iron formulas. Even with standard formulas, only a small amount of iron (about 5-10%) is absorbed from the formula. With a low-iron formula, they absorb very little iron at all.

In addition to the formula, I often recommend an iron-fortified rice cereal to be started at four months of age and additional foods started at six months of age, to prevent anemia.

Contrary to popular belief, there is not enough iron in either breast milk or formula to cause constipation.

If your infant was premature, she may need additional iron early on to prevent anemia. I recommend discussing this with your pediatrician.

Fluoride: Fluoride is a supplement that helps to prevent cavities in children. Additional fluoride is not routinely given to infants under 6 months of age, but may be given thereafter. Ask your pediatrician about fluoride recommendations in your area, because they vary based on the amount found in your local water supply.

Probiotics: The latest and greatest craze, these are supplements of live bacteria (the good kind) that are supposed to help balance the gut bacteria and aid in digestion. The research on probiotics is still somewhat early, but there is a suggestion that they may also aid in the reduction of some diseases such as asthma, as well as some food allergies. The current claim that probiotics decrease colic has not been fully borne out in the literature.

There are no current recommendations saying that infants should be placed on probiotics routinely. Some of the research is promising, but currently, I would recommend discussing it with your pediatrician prior to starting them.

(Wow! That last chapter was like mega long! You might want to get up and stretch for a bit or go get a cup of tea before continuing. Go ahead… I'll wait.)

Growing is Good

Whenit comes to evaluating the growth of an infant, we pediatricians are mainly interested in a few measurements. We follow height, weight, and head size, which give us a really good global indicator as to how a baby is doing.

During the first few weeks, the weight is probably the most important parameter that we follow, because the lack of weight gain can indicate a significant problem with your infant. However, height and head size can indicate problems as well, as I will discuss below.

Weight

When an infant is first born, it's common for them to lose up to 10% of their body weight by the first office visit, two to three days after discharge from the hospital. The first milestone in weight gain is that your newborn should be back to birth weight by two weeks of age. This gain is very important. It reassures us that the feeds are going well and your baby is heading in a good direction.

Next, we like to see your infant double his birth weight by four months of age and triple it by one year. These are rough waypoints for us to gauge proper growth in an infant. To get more precise, your pediatrician will use a growth chart. You should see this at each of your baby's checkups.

The growth chart demonstrates the ranges of normal growth of your infant, compared to other males or females of his or her age. We use these charts for height and head size as well, looking for trends that indicate normal healthy growth, or patterns that may suggest an underlying problem.

Length

This measurement is often not very accurate at first, because when your baby is first born, his little legs and feet are often drawn up into a flexed position. The accuracy depends solely on how well the labor and delivery personnel take the time to stretch the infant out straight to get the first measurement.

I don't lend too much credibility to the first few measurements, but over time with more plots on the growth chart, the height measurement becomes more accurate. Don't worry if you come to your first appointment with your pediatrician and she tells you that your baby is an inch shorter than when he was first born. It's most likely that your infant did not shrink, but simply didn't have the most accurate newborn measurement. The accuracy of these measurements will improve over time.

Head size

We measure the head size for two main reasons. We want to make sure that your baby's head is neither too big nor too small, relative to his height and weight. We also want to compare his head size with other newborns of the same gender. If a newborn infant's head is growing too quickly or too slowly, it can indicate a possible concern. As with the other measurements, we as pediatricians are more interested in trends than in any single measurement.

When it comes to the growth of your child, it's important to keep your newborn on a good check-up schedule with your pediatrician. We will follow your baby's growth with you and give you feedback on how your baby is growing.

Weight drop

As mentioned above, a weight drop after birth is normal in full-term babies. It's common for an infant to drop up to 10% of her birth weight in the first few days after birth. This weight drop happens because babies have excess water on board when they are born. This water holds them over until the mother's breast milk comes in, usually around the third day.

When newborns come in for their first follow-up visit from the hospital, I use the amount of weight reduction to help me gauge how well the feeds are going. By determining how much weight an infant has lost, I can get an indication of whether there may be a feeding problem. Greater weight loss tells me that we may have a bit of work to do to get your little one on the right track. The converse is true as well. If a newborn has lost an appropriate amount of weight, then I know that things are likely going well.

Remember that a drop in weight is normal at this first visit after leaving the hospital. If there are no feeding problems associated with your newborn, he should do fine.

Either way, your baby should be rechecked again around two weeks of age (sooner in some cases), to make sure that he has met the very important milestone of returning to birth weight.

Baby Care
Basics

L et's go over some basic newborn care and guidance. One key principle is simplicity. The more we do to our little ones, the more we tend to throw a wrench into things. In particular, this applies to the use of lotions, oils, powders, pastes, salves, Grandma's udder cream, and whatever else people feel that they must put on their baby. The simplest rule here is to minimize.

There's a good reason for this. Unlike our skin, a newborn baby's skin does not yet act very well as a barrier. That means that anything you put on your baby's skin can be absorbed much more readily into her skin, potentially leading to rashes or allergic reactions.

One thing many parents don't know is that babies are born with a dead layer of skin that needs to peel off. Because of this, it's not uncommon for babies' skin to appear dry, especially around the wrists and the ankles. The natural tendency is to want to put something on the dry skin to fix it, but it's not a dry skin condition, such as eczema. It will wash off over time as you start full-body bathing your infant. (Wait until after the cord falls off and the umbilical area dries out to do this.)

The baby is already naturally soft under this layer of dead skin. It's important to remember that it's just a dead layer that needs to shed off, not a dry, itchy skin condition that needs to be treated.

What happens if you do use lotions or oils on your baby? Most commonly, they block the sweat ducts and may lead to a heat rash or an allergic reaction.

I can usually tell when a parent is using baby oil on their infant, because they often have a very fine rash all over the body. Parents get worried about the rash and bring the baby into my office. The first question I ask is whether they are using oils or lotions. Usually, the answer is "yes." When they stop using the oil or lotion, the problem is solved.

Also, as a general rule, know that anything that smells real good (including a lot of baby products), is usually alcohol-based and therefore should be avoided. Your infant may not react well to these products.

Parents often ask when it will be OK to use lotions and oils. I generally tell them that the skin becomes more keratinized (fancy doctor talk for saying the skin acts as a barrier) by four months of age. If they would like to use some lotion after that, I wouldn't worry too much. However, I usually don't recommend much use of oils throughout infancy.

Powders

There are times and places for powders, but I don't routinely recommend them in the diaper area. They basically just mix with pee and poop to make paste.

The reasoning behind the use of powders is that they help keep an area dry. However, in your infant's case, you can achieve the same effect by opening up the diaper and air-drying, or by using a blow dryer SET ON THE COOL SETTING to quick-dry the diaper area.

There are times when we in the medical field will use powders, but they are usually medicated powders that we use in other places, such as the armpits and the neck areas in babies who might have a red, raw, "weeping" rash. If any of these areas appear to be getting irritated, I would recommend that you try the blow dryer trick with your infant several times a day. I usually don't have parents use powders in these areas because, if used too liberally, the infant could inhale small amounts into her lungs. That could be problematic.

People once thought that the use of corn starch in the diaper area could promote the growth of yeast. In recent studies, this has not been shown to be the case. However, I would not recommend the use of cornstarch powders in the neck or armpit areas because of the risk of inhalation into your infant's lungs.

If your baby has an irritated rash that isn't responding to your home care, it's best to take her to the pediatrician, rather than trying to treat it with products or home remedies. Remember, keep it simple.

Soaps

My approach to soaps is simple as well. Pick a mild soap. There are several products for babies on the market; Dove and Ivory are time-honored soaps. Be leery of the really good-smelling ones.

Once the cord is off and the belly button area is dry, you can wash your baby daily if you like. Just remember: their skin is sensitive. They aren't running around yet, getting into everything, and crawling through the doggy door every five minutes, so they don't get that dirty. I would minimize the amount of soap exposure on a daily basis, so as not to dry out their naturally soft skin. I usually recommend a bath with soap about once every three days. If you and your baby love the bonding aspect of bathing and would like to do it daily, that's no problem, but I would recommend just using plain warm water during these baths.

Diaper creams and ointments

This is an interesting subject for me. (Pediatricians are fascinated by this kind of stuff.) There are so many different products out there, yet every parent and pediatrician seems to have one favorite that he or she swears by.

My take is this: the function and purpose of a diaper cream or ointment is to act as a barrier on your baby's bottom. Its job is to protect the skin from the acidity of the vast numbers of pees and poops that will ensue. Therefore, find something that seems to work for you and use it.

For some unknown reason, one baby may respond to one but not another. You may just have to try a few. I tend to like the thick creams (usually with zinc oxide). I figure that, if it's impossible to get off of my fingers after applying it, it usually will do the same for your infant's bottom and act as a good barrier. Again, be leery of all the fancy concoctions out there that could complicate matters.

Diaper rash

These little guys will often get a red diaper area, because they poop and pee very frequently when starting out. When this happens, my first recommendation is getting air to the area.

Diapers block airflow and create a warm, dark, moist environment. This environment is a perfect setting for growing yeast—that's why babies get yeast skin infections in this area. It's also an environment that does not promote healing. Therefore, for most rashes in the diaper area, just getting cool or warm air in there is most helpful in resolving the rash.

One way to do that is to leave the diaper open or loose, to allow the area to breathe. You can also do the blow dryer trick described above. Using a diaper cream on your infant's bottom may also help.

Pediatricians have lots of little tricks when it comes to curing diaper rash, so you might want to ask yours. One trick that I like to use when an infant has a red, sore-looking bottom is to do a little sitz bath. This entails placing warm water in either the sink or a small plastic tub, just high enough to immerse the baby's bottom in. Put a couple of tablespoons of baking soda in the tub and mix thoroughly. Then sit your infant in the tub and hold him upright, so that only his bottom is immersed in the water. Support him there for about five minutes. Then take him out, pat him dry, blow-dry him, and apply your diaper cream to the area.

Another little trick that I use when the rash is weepy and the diaper cream won't stick is to apply a small amount of Maalox to the raw area. Let it air-dry, then seal it over with your diaper cream.

To help avoid possible problems, always use either unscented wipes or cool/warm cloths to clean your baby's bottom. Stay away from the scented stuff.

Cord care

It used to be that parents were told to put alcohol around the cord to keep it clean and prevent infections. However, it has been shown that alcohol does not prevent cord infections. In some cases, it may even delay the cord from falling off.

Again, I recommend simplicity. If we do nothing to this area, the cord will break down and usually fall off by itself by one to two weeks of age on average. All you need to do is keep it dry until it falls off and heals. In the meantime, sponge-bathe your baby and avoid getting the cord wet.

Caveat: If the cord has a small amount of bloody discharge around it or on the diaper or the baby's clothes, this is normal. Remember that there were three large blood vessels running through the cord. When the baby was born, the cord was clamped and cut. The remaining portion of the cord that was left behind may still retain some blood. As the cord breaks down, some of this residual blood mixes with the gelatinous substance of the cord and makes the cord appear bloody. This is normal.

What is not normal is if the cord is actively bleeding (dripping blood) or smells foul, or if the area around the cord is getting really red. If you see any of these things, contact your pediatrician.

Fingernail/toenail care

The fingernails are often long in newborn infants, and they grow quickly. They should be trimmed at least weekly.

You can use nail clippers, but you must be careful not to clip the end of the baby's finger. They do make safety clippers and scissors that you can buy to reduce the likelihood of injuring your baby, but you still need to be careful. Once the nails start to firm up a bit more, a soft emery board can be used to file the nails. This works well.

A good time to clip your infant's nails is during a feed (have someone else assist you) or while he's sleeping.

Circumcision

The current stance of the American Academy of Pediatrics is that circumcision is a very safe procedure and that the benefits outweigh the risks. It is a recommended procedure, but it's best that you as parents make the decision for your baby, based on your cultural, ethical, and religious beliefs.

The main benefits of circumcision are that it may help to reduce the incidence of urinary tract infections and the transmission of certain sexually transmitted diseases. It may also reduce the chance of penile cancer.

The most common risks that can be associated with circumcisions are bleeding, infection, and cosmetic problems (it doesn't look the way you want it to look after the procedure). Probably the most common complication that I see after circumcision is penile adhesion, where the remaining foreskin re-attaches to the head of the penis after the procedure. This is easily addressed.

All of these risks are rare, and again, they do not seem to outweigh the benefits of circumcision.

The procedure is generally tolerated very well. I typically use what is called a penile nerve block to control pain. This is done by injecting lidocaine (anesthetic) at the base of the penis prior to the procedure. This numbs the penis for about two to four hours.

You would be surprised how well infants tolerate the procedure, from a pain standpoint. They are mainly just mad at being restrained for the procedure, and often calm right down as soon as they are picked up afterwards. For pain control at home after the circumcision, I recommend acetaminophen. However, it is very rare to have significant pain after the procedure.

There are different methods for performing the circumcision. The two most common are the Gomco and Plastibell methods. For both of these procedures, the outcome is the same. Basically, the difference between the two main types is that the Gomco procedure allows for the foreskin to be excised (removed) at the time of the procedure. With the Plastibell procedure, a bell-shaped piece of plastic is placed over the head of the penis and secured very tightly with a ligature (string), cutting off the circulation to the foreskin. This causes the foreskin to fall off over a period of three to seven days.

For more information on the specifics of the procedures, you can consult a big reference book or ask your provider how he or she performs the procedure. Performing a circumcision usually takes only 10 to 15 minutes in the office.

Care of the penis right after the circumcision will vary by pediatrician. I have parents wash the site daily with a mild soap, such as Dove or Ivory, and place Vaseline around the surgical site until it heals in about seven to 10 days.

Once the circumcision is healed, there is really no additional care needed. Wash the area as you would any other area of the body at regular bath times.

Care of the uncircumcised penis

The care for an uncircumcised penis is very easy and low-maintenance. Just clean the outside of the penis at regular bathing times. The foreskin does not usually pull back before one to three years of age. At that time, it will be more important to pull back the foreskin and wash around the head of the penis to keep it clean and prevent infection, but until then, just leave it alone. Do not pull back the foreskin of a newborn infant. You may cause bleeding, and the foreskin can get entrapped or "stuck" behind the head of the penis.

If you have any questions regarding the cleaning and maintenance of your newborn's penis, contact your pediatrician.

Sleep

"People who say that they sleep like
a baby usually don't have one."

—Leo J. Burke

At first, newborns sleep 16 hours a day or more. They tend to wake every two to three hours on average to feed and then go back to sleep. You may even find that your baby can reflexively feed while snoozing.

Your baby is doing most of her growing while sleeping. Therefore, she will require a lot of sleep time at first. Most babies also move around a lot in their sleep, grunting, straining, and sometimes giving out a brief cry. This restless pattern is normal and will change as she gets older.

Sleep position
It's very simple: place your newborn on his back ONLY. Do not

place an infant on his side to sleep and NEVER on his tummy to sleep. Studies show that infants who have died from sudden infant death syndrome (SIDS) were most often placed on their sides or their tummies to sleep. By placing our newborns on their backs to sleep, we have seen a dramatic 40-50% reduction in the number of deaths related to SIDS.

Some factors that have been shown to increase the incidence of SIDS in newborn babies are:

- over-dressing or over-bundling an infant before sleep
- sleeping in bed with the parent
- exposure to cigarette smoke

On the other hand, the use of pacifiers has been shown to decrease SIDS risk.

When I recommend placing an infant on his or her back to sleep, the most common question that I get from parents is, "What if my baby spits up and chokes?" It's a good question, because babies do spit up a lot. However, newborn infants are also pretty good at guarding their airways from liquid being sucked into their lungs. I remind parents that infants are being placed on their backs to sleep every night all over the world, but when was the last time you heard on the news about an infant choking to death on breast milk or formula?

Can babies spit up and potentially suck liquid into their lungs (aspirate) while lying on their backs? Yes, it is possible, but we very rarely see this happen. The risk of SIDS far outweighs this slight risk. That's why it's still recommended to place your baby on her back to sleep.

Sometimes, as a result of placing your infant on her back to sleep, she may get a little flattening to the back or the side of her head. This can be decreased by not leaving your baby lying down for long periods throughout the day when she is not sleeping. Also, you can help even things out by rotating the baby's head to the opposite side of the flattening when you put her down. If you have questions regarding the shape of your baby's head, ask your pediatrician.

Bedding

On the subject of bedding, again, I recommend keeping it simple. Besides a firm mattress with a tight fitted sheet, your infant should not have anything other than a thin receiving blanket in his sleeping area.

You may see lots of cool little bedding sets that you could get for your infant, to match the room and complete your whole nursery theme. There are lots of nice blankets, pillows, and other things that you can place in your baby's crib or bassinet. I have one word for you: Don't. Loose bedding or bulky bedding of any kind can pose a risk to your infant. Your baby could become entrapped and/or suffocate.

You should not put any bumpers, stuffed animals, or other items that could pose a risk to your newborn in the crib or bassinet. As big people, we prefer pillows to sleep on, but your infant does not need one. Simple is best.

Co-sleeping

The term co-sleeping is used when a parent chooses to bring the baby into bed to sleep with them. Although this can be a risk factor for SIDS, there are many cultures around the world that practice co-sleeping as a norm. Without additional risk factors such as a parent being under the influence of alcohol, drugs, or medications, or being an abnormally deep sleeper, the risk of smothering an infant is very low. However, an infant can still get entrapped in loose bedding or push his face into a sleeping parent, which could increase the risk of suffocation.

In the case of co-sleeping, there is not a lot of evidence to support an opinion in either direction, but I want to make sure you know the risks. As a pediatrician, I feel that it's important to inform parents of potential risks to their infant, no matter what choice they make. This way, you can make a more educated decision for yourself.

Swaddling

When babies are inside the womb, they're in a pretty comfortable environment. They're enclosed, and they feel safe in their little swimming pool.

Once born, they're suddenly part of this vast open space called "the world." They feel exposed and vulnerable. What they have known for all of their brief lives has now changed.

Given this, it's only natural to want to gravitate back to the comfort of what they have known. So, in essence, your little one will be most comfortable in any setting that mimics the environment of the womb. One of the ways that a newborn can re-create the feeling of being enclosed and safe is to be swaddled.

When first born, your infant may be comforted by swaddling. As your baby starts to adjust to her new environment, you may see that she doesn't want to be swaddled any longer.

This is the case for many infants, but there are still some infants who like to be swaddled beyond the newborn period. This doesn't create much of a problem if it is not prolonged. However, we are now finding that prolonged swaddling can predispose some infants toward hip dysplasia (where their hips don't grow into their hip sockets properly).

Because of this risk, it is currently recommended that if you swaddle your baby beyond the newborn period (usually about a month), you can wrap her arms, but you should leave her legs free to move unrestricted. You can even buy infant swaddling blankets made just for this purpose.

Dermatology 101

I n this chapter, I will give you a crash course in pediatric dermatology (the study of the skin). When you are done with
this part of the book, you will know more about newborn
baby skin findings than a third-year medical student. However,
pay close attention: there will be a test.

Why devote an entire chapter to conditions of a newborn's
skin? Well, as you will soon see, there are quite a few skin conditions that can arise over the first month of your newborn's life.
Most of them are normal.

The skin is the largest organ of the human body. It's also the
most visible. That means any rash, redness, raised bumps, or
perceived abnormality of the skin is clearly visible to a parent's
scrutinizing eye.

I find that a lot of parental concerns and questions center
around the way their baby's skin looks soon after birth and
through the first month, so I want to give you a crash course on
what's normal. That way, when your little one comes into the
world, you will be an expert.

Dry skin

Your baby will probably be born with dry and peeling skin. This is normal for newborns, and you should know that it's not an itchy, dry skin condition. It's just dead skin.

We all have dead skin. It's just that, for us, the outer layers of our skin are constantly sloughed off as we bathe and go about our day. For babies, that doesn't happen in the womb, because they're floating freely in liquid. There's little or no friction or rubbing to remove these old skin cells.

With no mechanical way to slough off the skin, it just stays where it is. Then, when the baby is born, this excess skin gets exposed to the air and dries out.

The tendency is to want to put lotions on the baby. After all, if our skin looked like that, we would pile on the lotion. But for your newborn, there is really nothing specific that you need to do to "fix" the dry skin. It will wash off over time as you give your baby full-body baths, after the cord falls off and dries out. Underneath this dry layer, you have a naturally soft baby,

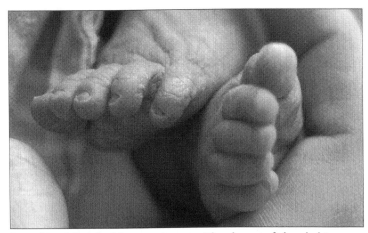

Dry skin: Most babies are born with a layer of dead skin.
Photo © iStock.com/StevieS

so lotions are not necessary.

You may also notice your infant's lips peeling, appearing as if the infant had chapped lips. This, too, is normal. It's just part of the dead layer of skin that needs to slough off.

When they see this, many parents become concerned that the baby isn't getting enough liquids, and they want to give the baby water. There is no need to give water to your newborn baby, and doing so can actually cause problems. Remember, just like so many other things going on with your newborn baby, peeling lips are normal. The friction from sucking will remove the dead skin. There's no need for you to do anything about it.

On the other hand, you may see your baby's skin crack, fissure, or even bleed a little or form a scab, especially in the wrist and ankle areas. If you see that, you can apply a little bit of Vaseline several times daily to prevent these areas from bothering your infant.

Newborn rash

For many babies, a rash will pop up within the first 24 to 48 hours after birth. Pediatricians find it kind of cool, but new parents often get concerned because it looks like mosquito bites. Parents will often worry that something is causing these "bites" on their baby. There is no reason to worry—nothing is biting your baby. It's just a rash.

This rash has a red base to it and most often a raised white or yellowish center. These lesions or bumps are migratory, meaning that they move to different places on the body. If you watch them now, they will disappear and pop up somewhere else later.

They look like they might itch or otherwise be bothersome to your baby, but they are totally normal. In about two to four weeks' time, they'll simply disappear.

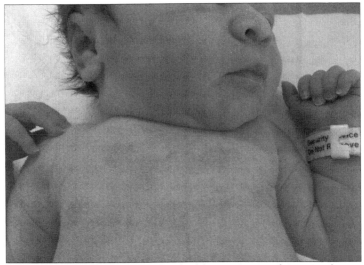

Newborn rash: a rash that looks like mosquito bites is also common for newborn babies.

Photo reprinted with permission from Meghan E Hughes, MD, Naval Medical Center San Diego, published by Medscape Reference, 2014, available at: http://emedicine.medscape.com/article/1110731-overview.

Angel Kisses and Stork Bites

These cute names are used to describe the red birth marks that are commonly found on about 40% of newborn infants. These result from the very superficial collections of capillaries (tiny little blood vessels) in your baby's skin. Since capillaries carry the baby's red blood cells, these birth marks are red in color.

The "Angel kisses" appear most commonly over the eyelids. These red birthmarks can also appear in the center of the forehead and around the nose. They tend to flush and get more red when the baby is warm (such as during a warm bath) or when crying. With time, these types of birth marks often disappear completely or fade until they're only slightly visible.

If you turn your baby over and look at the nape of the neck, you may see a superficial red birthmark here as well. This is

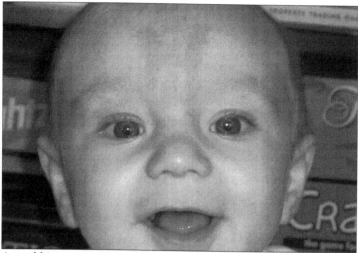

Angel kisses: a common birthmark that will fade over time.

Photo © Alyssa Aarhaus of From Military to Mom
(alyssamarieaarhaus.com). Reprinted with permission.

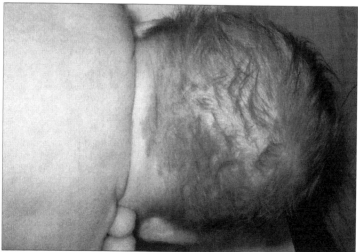

Stork bite: another common birthmark.

called a "stork bite." It too will often flush when your infant is warm or crying.

This birthmark may extend up onto the back of the scalp. The big difference with this birthmark versus the "angel kisses" is that "stork bites" may become permanent 25-40% of the time. This is nothing to be concerned about. Even if it persists, the mark is often covered by the hairline as your baby grows. Lots and lots of people have these "stork bites" but don't even realize it because they're covered.

There are other types of red birthmarks that an infant can be born with. Most commonly, these are called hemangiomas. They can be found anywhere on the body and may get bigger or become raised over time as the baby grows.

Most hemangiomas will go away by the time a child reaches school age. They are most commonly non-problematic, but depending on their location, they may need to be followed more closely. Your pediatrician will be quite adept and knowledgeable when it comes to these birthmarks, as they are very common.

Another type of red birthmark is called a "port wine stain."

Hemangioma: another common birthmark.

Photo ©
iStock.com/Lawrence-
Sawyer

These are far less common than the types we've mentioned so far. Port wine stains appear flat and much more extensive. They're a deeper purple and often extend over the face and neck on one side. Port wine stains are permanent, and they can be associated with underlying problems. Again, your pediatrician will be knowledgeable in this area and can make sure that your infant is taken care of properly.

Mongolian spotting

These "spots" or birthmarks are most commonly found in darker-skinned infants, including African American, Asian, and Hispanic infants. However, they may be seen in any infant of any skin color.

These birthmarks are dark, almost purple. They're most often found on the baby's bottom and just above, on the lower

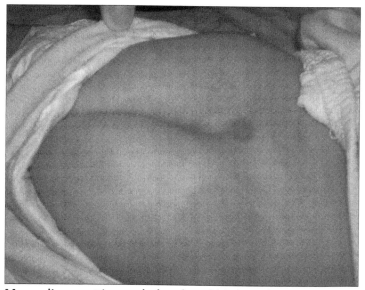

Mongolian spotting: a dark-colored birthmark sometimes mistaken for bruising.

back. However, these marks may appear anywhere on the body and can be quite large. They're not harmful, and they often lighten up over time. Most will disappear by two to three years of age, although some may become permanent.

Parents and other care providers often mistake these birthmarks for bruises, but as you become familiar with your baby's skin, you will notice that these birthmarks don't change. They will be with your infant for a while. No worries—this is normal.

Milia

Milia are little collections of small white pinpoint bumps that are most often found over the bridge of the nose, chin, and cheeks. These little lesions are the result of blocked skin pores. They will open up and go away over time by themselves. There is no need to do anything to them.

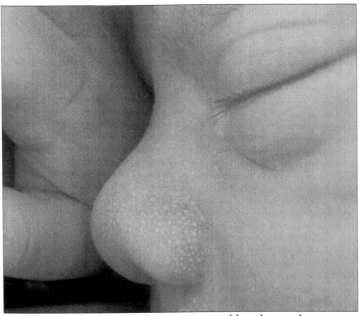

Milia (milk spots): white bumps caused by clogged pores.

Photo by user: Serephine / Wikimedia Commons / Public Domain

Miliaria

Otherwise known as "heat rash" or "prickly heat," these are small red bumps that are usually present over the chest and the back of an infant. This rash is often a result of being too warm or being over-bundled. It usually clears up in a few days.

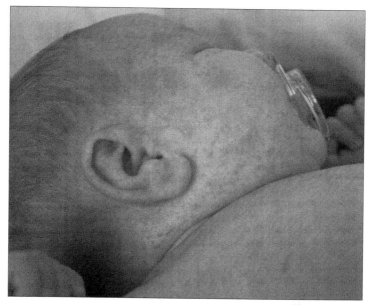

Miliaria (heat rash or prickly heat): a rash that usually clears up within a few days.

Photo by Jessica Reid of Journey to Crunchville (http://journeytocrunchville.wordpress.com). Used with permission.

Pustular melanosis

This is a newborn rash that is associated with very small blister-like bumps that appear at birth or soon after, usually over the infant's trunk. These small bumps open up and scab over, then turn dark and appear much like little freckles over the body. They usually disappear after a few weeks.

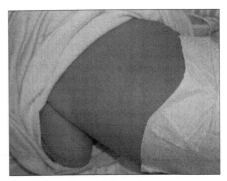

Pustular Melanosis: a rash that appears as small bumps that initially look like blisters and later look like freckles.

Photo by Dr. Ari Brown, from the book *Baby 411*. Used with permission.

Neonatal acne (baby pimples)

Another common rash is neonatal acne, otherwise known as "baby pimples." This rash doesn't quite present right at birth, but often develops slowly when an infant is between two to four weeks of age. It appears as small pimples that are usually located mainly on the cheeks, although they can also appear on the upper chest and back.

These little pimples are the result of maternal hormones that are passed directly to the baby from the mom while the baby is in the womb. These hormones have the same effect on the skin as when adolescents go through puberty (minus the emotional changes). Sometimes, the pimples can get quite heavy and look bad for the baby pictures, but they don't bother the infant. They're not itchy or irritating, so treatment is often not necessary. If you get concerned about the rash, ask your pediatrician. The acne usually dissipates between one to three months of age.

Cradle Cap

Speaking of hormone-related rashes, there is another common rash that usually develops over time (usually after two to four weeks). This rash is seborrhea, commonly known as cradle cap. Parents often mistake this rash to be called cradle "crap," which always makes me smile. The correct term is cradle cap.

This rash leads to thick yellow-brown scales on the scalp and/or eyebrows. The rash looks dry, but it is actually a "greasy"

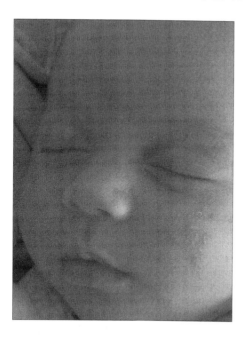

Neonatal acne: pimples that often appear two to four weeks after birth due to maternal hormones.

Photo by selbst erstellt (Fragegeist). Fragegeist at de.wikipedia [Public domain], from Wikimedia Commons

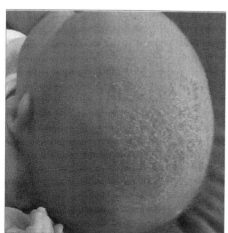

Cradle cap: a scaly rash on the baby's scalp.

Photo by user: Starfoxy / Wikimedia Commons / CC-BY-SA-3.0

type of rash.

Like the others, this rash will go away over time as the maternal hormones disappear from the baby's bloodstream. You don't need to do anything for it. However, if you want to address it, you can apply some baby oil on the scalp one hour before bathing. Doing this will soften the scales. Then, during the bath, you can lightly scrub with a soft bristle brush or washcloth to try to remove the scales. The key here is to NOT leave the baby oil on the scalp. If you leave the oil on the scalp, it can block your infant's sweat ducts and cause a heat rash.

If this doesn't quite do the trick, and the rash persists or gets worse, you can use an anti-dandruff shampoo twice weekly for five minutes.

In addition to these treatments, you can also use some 1% hydrocortisone cream, which is available over the counter. You may use this on your infant's scalp once daily for no more than seven days, to see if it will help resolve the scaling.

Caveat: Please don't use baby oil all over your infant's body. It works great to make your baby smell good, but it blocks the sweat ducts and usually leads to heat rash.

Skin Conditions that Cause Concern

While all of the skin issues we've just covered are normal and not harmful, that's not true for everything. If you see any type of blisters or any lesions that appear to be vesicles (containing fluid), you need to bring those to your pediatrician's attention immediately. Some lesions can be associated with infections that can be very dangerous to a newborn baby, so you need to get those checked out.

Fingernails and toenails

Soon after birth, it's common for an infant's fingernails to be soft and long. They have never been cut before, so they may need a trim (see the section under baby basics).

Soon, they will dry out, which can lead to your infant scratching her face a lot. This is because she instinctively draws her hands into a flexed position and constantly keeps them close to her face.

The nails grow quickly. In addition to keeping them trimmed constantly, you can put the little hand mitts on her to keep her from scratching herself. I usually recommend that a parent not use these little mitts beyond the first month, though. If you keep using the mitts, you take away a very important sense from your baby: the sensation of touch. Your baby needs to experience her world through touch, just like we do. We wouldn't like wearing gloves all day every day, and neither will she, so be vigilant on the nail trimming and minimal on the mitts.

Just as your newborn's fingernails may need to be cut very soon after birth, so may her toenails. Trim them as needed.

When it comes to toenails in newborn infants, the most common question I get is, "Why does my baby have ingrown toenails?" For many newborns, the skin on the sides of their toenails grows up and over the nails, thus making the nails appear small and ingrown. The reason for this is because, when your infant was inside of you in her little swimming pool, the nails were very soft and flimsy. This allowed the soft skin surrounding her nails to grow over top of the nail somewhat, slightly obscuring the nails.

This appearance is normal, and once your infant's nails get firmer, they will grow out on either side and take on a more normal appearance. It can take months (sometimes even years) for the nails to firm up to a point where they don't appear flimsy anymore. Have patience, and time will prevail.

Pediatric Dermatology Pop Quiz

Match each skin condition to its description:

___ Newborn rash   A. Not cradle crap

___ Mongolian spots   B. Looks like small mosquito bites

___ Baby pimples   C. Often found in darker skinned infants

___ Cradle cap   D. Red birthmark on the eyelids

___ Angel kiss   E. Neonatal acne

Congratulations! You have just finished your first course in pediatric dermatology. The answers to your quiz are upside-down below. If you got all five answers right, you are brilliant, off to a great start and as smart as a first-year pediatric resident. If you answered three to four questions correctly, good job—you are as smart as a fourth-year medical student. If you only got zero to two answers right, you might need to go back and review, but have no worries—you're still smarter than a third-year medical student.

Answers to quiz: 1.B, 2.C, 3.E, 4.A, 5.D

Breast Bud Swelling, Newborn Periods, and Witch's Milk

Remember when we talked about neonatal acne (above), and I told you about maternal hormones that were passed to your baby while she was still inside of you? Well, besides those hormones affecting your baby's skin and causing baby pimples, there are other parts of your baby's body that may respond to these hormones as well.

If you have a baby girl, within the first few days after birth, you may see a little bit of blood or white mucous that comes from the vaginal opening. Many parents find this quite unsettling. I reassure them that it's not only normal, but it also tells me that their newborn baby girl was born with all of her normal anatomy to have periods in the future. In short, she is healthy.

The "newborn period" or pseudo-menses will usually last only two or three days. After that, it will disappear until she starts her true period when she is older. If the newborn period lasts more than three days, I would recommend that you contact your pediatrician.

Another hormone-sensitive area of the newborn's body is the breast tissue. Whether a baby is male or female, this tissue responds to maternal hormones, possibly leading to swelling of the breast tissue. In some babies, this causes the breast to form a firm disc underneath the nipple. If this occurs, it usually happens about two weeks after birth.

In addition to the enlargement that can occur in the breast tissue, the infant can also make milk (otherwise known as witch's milk). This milk can actually be expressed from the nipple.

When I show this to parents in the office, it usually concerns them. After all, most of us wouldn't expect our newborn infant to be able to produce milk. However, this is normal and no cause for alarm. The baby only makes a drop of milk here or there, and nothing needs to be done about it. After two to four weeks, the maternal hormones usually start to decrease in the baby's bloodstream and the breast bud swelling and milk production will stop.

In some cultures, they manually express the milk from the baby's breast, believing that this will lead to good breast shape in adulthood. There are no facts to support this practice, and it can lead to infection, so please do not express milk from your baby's breast.

A little trivia: The term "witch's milk" comes from folklore. People once believed that if an infant produced milk, it was because the infant was unwanted. The milk produced by these unwanted infants would be taken up and used to nourish the "familiar spirits"—supernatural assistants that helped witches perform their magic.

No worries, though. Through the wonders of science, the myth of witch's milk has long since been disproven. We can all rest easy knowing that your infant is normal and healthy, and witchcraft has nothing to do with it.

In addition to pseudo-menses, baby acne, and breast tissue swelling, you may observe a few other hormone-related findings soon after birth. For girls, the labia may appear swollen and enlarged. For boys, the scrotum may appear darkly pigmented. Both of these findings eventually resolve as the maternal hormones disappear from your baby's system.

Eye have a question

Believe it or not, I get a lot of questions about newborns' eyes. Parents often want to know whether their baby can see, how to classify her eye color, and why her eyes cross. I've assembled the answers to the most common questions in this short chapter for you. I hope you will find it helpful and informative.

Eye color

There are basically four eye colors to choose from: blue, green, gray, and brown. Your infant's ultimate eye color will be a variation of one of these colors.

Usually, the eye color you see at six months is what you get. However, your baby's eyes may continue shading throughout the first year before you know the ultimate intensity of the iris color. If an infant is going to have brown eyes, they will often shift to this color earlier, between two and three months of age. Infants who are going to have blue, green, or gray eyes will often progress to their respective color by six months of life.

How far can my baby see?

Most babies can see relatively clearly for about eight to 15 inches—about the distance from the mother's breast to the mother's face. Babies are instinctively attracted to faces and will start to recognize yours soon after birth. They also like alternating patterns of black and white or red and black, as are often found in infant-stimulation toys.

The vision gets better over time, and so does control of the eye muscles. By about two months of age, your baby will be able to see about two or three feet clearly and give you a smile when you come into her view. At this age, she will be able to fix on your face but usually will not be able to follow you or track you as you move. That ability develops around four months of age.

Eye-crossing

In the newborn infant, brief inward eye-crossing is usually normal. It reflects the fact that your infant has not yet learned to use both eyes together. As a result of this, you may see that they wander somewhat randomly. This coordination usually improves between two to three months of age. At or beyond this age, you should not see any eye-crossing. If you think you may be seeing one or both of your infant's eyes crossing or appearing abnormal, consult your pediatrician so that your infant can be further evaluated.

Scleral hemorrhages

Scleral hemorrhages are basically popped capillaries (tiny blood vessels) within the white areas of your baby's eyes. They appear as small collections of blood that can be seen on the white parts of the eyes on either side of the iris (the colored portion of the eye).

These small hemorrhages are usually seen in one eye, but they may occur in both. They come from the pressure that is exerted on your infant during the birth process, which can be quite intense. This increase in pressure basically "pops" the tiny blood vessels of the eye. This same thing can also happen to moms, from the pressure of pushing while in labor. Either way, they are totally painless and usually resolve on their own over a few weeks.

Blocked tear duct

Very commonly, parents will bring their newborn infant into the office, reporting that "his eye looks infected—he has this yellow gunk coming out of it." Even though we are instinctively trained to think that "yellow gunk" is infection, that's not always true. In the case of your newborn infant's eyes, it is most often a sign of a blocked tear duct.

Oftentimes, the tear duct of a newborn infant is not fully opened at birth. This can occur in one eye or both eyes, but it is most commonly seen in one.

Our tears naturally drain from our eyes through a small sac in the corner of the eye and then down the side of the nose through a duct that opens within the nose. This is why your nose runs when you cry. In newborns, oftentimes the duct is not yet fully opened on one side or the other. As a result, the tears don't drain as they normally would.

When this occurs, the components that make up the tears are exposed to the air and thicken up into a yellow-looking discharge that often appears on the outside of the eye. As a parent, you may see that the baby's eye is crusted shut from time to time (usually the morning). A warm, wet washcloth can be used to remove the discharge. The discharge is most often not associated with infection, even though it looks yellow.

With a blocked tear duct, you should see that the white part of the eye remains white and there is no redness or inflammation to the eye. You should not see swelling in the eyelid or thick green discharge. Redness, swelling, and green discharge can be signs of infection. If you observe these things, or if you're unsure, contact your pediatrician immediately.

Treatment for blocked tear ducts: Contrary to what is often believed, antibiotic eye drops or ointments are not effective in treating a blocked tear duct, since this is not an infection. It's a mechanical obstruction.

Most commonly, the mainstay of care is keeping the eye discharge cleaned out. However, massaging the corner eye sac (called the nasolacrimal sac) and the duct (the nasolacrimal duct) may help in opening the duct sooner. This massage technique is performed by using your finger to massage in a circular motion around the inner corner of the eye near the nose, and then running your finger down the side of the baby's nose from the inner corner of the eye down to the tip of the nose on the affected side. Although it's not absolutely necessary, I usually recommend doing this about three times a day at diaper changes.

It's important to know that the ducts most often will simply open by themselves without a lot of intervention on our part. Rarely, if the duct doesn't open by about 10 months of age, the baby may have to be seen by an eye specialist, who might consider opening the duct. However, this is rare. You and your provider will make that decision together if it is warranted.

Odds and Ends

"The things that make me different
are the things that make me, Me!"

—*A.A. Milne / Winnie the pooh*

Joint popping: It is common for parents to ask about their infant's joints popping. Parents often report either the sound or the feeling of a large joint "popping" when the infant is picked up. This is because pregnant women produce a hormone called **relaxin** that works on the ligaments of the pelvis, allowing them to relax and accommodate the passage of the infant through the birth canal. This hormone is passed from the mother to the baby while the infant is in the womb. It has the same relaxing effects on the baby's joints, causing them to make a popping sound or sensation that can be felt. This sound or feeling can be in any joint, but it's most commonly observed in the shoulder, knees, and back. The "popping" is non-painful and non-harmful. As the hormones dissipate from the baby's body over time, this laxity will decrease.

Blood in newborn stools: During the first few days after delivery, you might see blood in the stools of a newborn baby. Most often, this is a result of blood swallowed during the birth process or blood that was sucked and swallowed during breastfeeding. Blood also can be seen in the stools if your infant is allergic to the cow's milk or soy protein in the formula or in the breast milk. The blood associated most commonly with cow's milk or soy allergies is usually seen several weeks after birth, though.

For good measure, if you see blood in the stools of your newborn, I would recommend making your pediatrician aware of it.

Retractile testicles: Newborn infant males can retract their testicles up and out of the scrotum, just like puppies. As long as both testicles are found down in the scrotum at birth, it's ok if they tend to wander up and down at first. They ultimately should settle into the scrotum over time.

Urate crystals: It is not uncommon within the first few days to see a somewhat pasty, pinkish-orange substance in the diaper. Not to be confused with blood in the stools or blood from a "newborn period," the crystals are usually located more towards the front of the diaper.

This comes from your baby peeing a substance called urate. Urate consists of crystals that are actually very pretty under a microscope. Initially, they are common and no cause for alarm. They should resolve soon after birth.

If they do not, or if they reoccur, then they may be a sign of impending dehydration, indicating that your infant needs more fluids. If they do not soon resolve, or if they return after initially going away, you should ask your pediatrician about them.

Babies are noisy: Parents are always asking me if the sounds that their baby makes are normal. I often tell them that infants spend a good amount of their time grunting, straining, and intermittently fussing around. They often make sighing sounds, congestion sounds, and high-pitched sounds when breathing inwards. For the most part, these sounds are normal. Sometimes, they may be purposeful; other times, they're random. You will hear these sounds very frequently throughout early infancy.

Milk tongue vs. thrush: Milk tongue is seen when the breast milk or formula deposits in the tiny crevices of the tongue. It appears as a thin white coating on the tongue. It's not harmful, and there's really not much that needs to be done for it. Thrush, on the other hand, is actually a yeast overgrowth that establishes in the mouth due to microscopic breaks in the mucous membranes of the infant's mouth. These breaks are caused by the sucking action of the baby when he eats. The yeast that lives in the mouth seeds these breaks and causes an overgrowth.

Thrush appears more raised, thick, and yellow-white than milk tongue. It has a somewhat "furry" appearance on the tongue, showing up as white patches on the inner cheeks and lips. As opposed to residual formula or breast milk, thrush cannot be wiped away with a wet washcloth.

To try to prevent thrush, you can clean your baby's mouth out with a wet washcloth. You'll want to do this several times daily after feeding, to remove the thin film of food that stays in your infant's mouth. Otherwise, this film can become a food source, helping the yeast to establish and grow.

It's also important to keep nipples and pacifiers as clean as possible, so that they don't harbor residual yeast. Regular soap and water or the dishwasher will be sufficient for this.

If you feel that your baby has thrush, you should visit your pediatrician. Your baby may need an anti-yeast medicine (most commonly Nystatin) to treat the infection.

Vaccines: There is a lot that could be said on the subject of vaccines—so much, in fact, that it could be the subject of an entire book (future project). There's a tremendous amount of hype and misinformation out there in the "infosphere." Frankly, a large part of it is plain wrong and serves no purpose other than to propagate fear. It simply comes down to this: there has never been any single invention known to mankind that has saved more lives than vaccines... None. As a matter of fact, vaccines have only gotten safer and safer, while we (the medical world) have gotten very good at eradicating deadly and debilitating diseases, or at least keeping them in check. Unfortunately, we've gotten so good that the public at large has all but forgotten the devastating effects of the measles, whooping cough, diphtheria, polio, and other such diseases.

As a result of this new age, parents now often "shop" their vaccines, picking and choosing the ones they want to give, often based on word of mouth and pseudo-research. What amazes me most about this "research" is that, although parents can tell me all kinds of reasons why they don't want a particular vaccine, they can never tell me anything about the truly devastating diseases that they are deciding not to vaccinate against. For some reason, they don't seem to look up the clinical presentation of a child with measles, diphtheria, polio, or whooping cough. If they did, I think these conversations might be very different.

It's vitally important for you to know that, due to this increasing trend towards non-vaccination or semi-vaccination of our children, we are starting to see numerous holes in the fabric of vaccination across our country. As a result, we are realizing a resurgence of these totally preventable, deadly diseases. For example, at the time of this writing (2014), there has been a tenfold increase in the number of whooping cough cases across our nation. Previously, this disease had largely been kept in check through vaccination.

Remember, these diseases that we continually strive to prevent are not gone in nature. They are only controlled by the continual, unrelenting practice of vaccination. As soon as we stop vaccinating, they return. We've already seen that, and we'll continue to see it as people opt out of vaccinations. Please don't let misinformation lead you to put your child at risk.

If you have questions on the subject of vaccines, I suggest that you go to reputable web sites such as the American Academy of Pediatrics (aap.org) or the Centers for Disease Control (cdc.gov). Or, if you like, you can discuss them with your pediatrician. After all, we are experts on the matter, considering that we give vaccinations on a daily basis, year after year, worldwide.

Please remember that we pediatricians dedicate our lives to the health and well-being of all children, and specifically your child. Vaccination is at the core of this care. I believe vaccination is paramount in safeguarding one's child against the possible perils that Mother Nature has to offer.

Baby fun facts (BFFs)

BFF: Infants have a natural tendency to like sweets as opposed to bitter or sour tastes.

BFF: Infants can see light, dark, and shadows at birth, but most can't appreciate a full range of color.

BFF: In newborns, the xiphoid process (the little pointy bone at the end of the breast bone) often flips upwards, because it is not fully made of bone yet and therefore is soft. This often creates a little bump at the end of the breast bone in the center of the chest. This finding is normal and goes away in time.

BFF: Since infants' tummy muscles are weak, their abdomens often protrude out to the sides, especially after eating or when the infant is sleeping and in his most relaxed state. The tummy may also appear bigger on one side versus the other (asymmetric). This is because the liver on the right side of the tummy is bigger than the spleen on the left. However, when the tummy is full of food and/or air, you may see the tummy appear more prominent on the left.

BFF: In addition to an asymmetric tummy, some infants will have an out-pouching of the midline of their abdomen, most commonly noted when pushing, straining, or crying. This is not an umbilical hernia (belly button hernia), which comes out just above the belly button. Instead, this out-pouching is longer and farther above the belly button. It represents a weakness in the middle of the abdomen, which will resolve when the infant gets a bit older and the tummy muscles tighten. This finding is called a diastasis recti and is normal.

BFF: Believe it or not, the color of poop is a very common concern for parents. When a baby is first born, the poop is a thick, dark green (almost black) gelatinous poop called meconium. As food starts making its way through the gastro-intestinal tract, this thick stool will change to a more liquid green version (transitional stools), and then ultimately to a bright or pale yellow stool with small formed seed-like components. These findings are normal, and any shades of stool from green to brown to yellow are normal.

On the other hand, if you see bright red stools consistent with blood, or stools that appear white and seem to have no color, those are not normal. If you see either of those types of stools, contact your pediatrician.

BFF: Does my baby have Attention Deficit Hyperactivity Disorder (ADHD)? I just threw this question in here for fun. When writing this book, I asked my physician assistants for some examples of questions posed to them by parents. One of my assistants submitted this question, which not only did I find humorous, but I think it illustrates very well that there are no limitations to the questions and concerns that a parent might have when it comes to the wellbeing of their newborn baby. (Although your baby might exhibit traits of ADHD such as a complete lack of focus, impulsive crying, and an inability to complete simple tasks without constant redirection, it's not ADHD. That's just how babies are.)

BFF: Parents will often remark about how rapidly their

baby's heart beats. Infants' hearts beat faster than ours for a reason. As adults, our hearts are stronger, so they beat slowly but with more force than a newborn's heart. Since infants' hearts aren't as strong, they instead beat faster to get the blood to all the vital areas of the body. The rate slows as one grows through childhood into adulthood.

BFF: Newborn infants do not need juice to help them poop. Remember, since babies aren't eating big chunks of food, they don't need to go all the time. Please save the juice until after 10 months of age, or for times when your pediatrician might recommend it.

BFF: When it comes to piercing your baby's ears, there is no one ideal age that's better than any other. On the other hand, in my personal experience, I see more complications and infections when earrings are placed in toddlers and young children, as opposed to early infants. Older children tend to play with the new earrings more, which lends toward a higher frequency of infections.

If you decide to get your baby's ears pierced, I would recommend taking her to a place that is regulated by the local health department and that has a lot of experience in performing ear piercings on infants. I also recommend 18- to 22-karat gold posts for the first set of earrings, as these will be the least likely to cause an allergic reaction.

The End is just the Beginning

"Today's special moments are tomorrow's memories."

—*Genie*, Aladdin

Well, that's about it. We have reached the end of what I hope has been a relatively painless and informative journey. I hope I've given you a practical understanding of how your baby works and how to approach her care. I've tried to cut through the rhetoric and distill the vast quantities of available information into a simple, practical, common-sense instruction manual for you.

Throughout my time in practice as a pediatrician, I've seen so many parents deeply concerned about how to approach and care for their newborn babies. They bring them in to me soon after birth, often with a complete look of bewilderment on their faces. This look, which I have seen for so many years, is why I have written this book. This book has been designed with all parents in mind, first-timers and veterans alike. If I have helped you to have a better understanding of your baby and allayed some of your fears, then my time has been well spent and a true joy.

I know that parents are always going to have questions and concerns when it comes to the wellbeing of their children. If you didn't, I might just be out of a job. But the mere fact that you have taken the time to learn about your child is a testament to the budding devotion, love, and care that I have found to be characteristic of any great parent. Pay attention to your baby and your instincts, and utilize your pediatrician. You'll do fine. I have complete faith in your abilities as a parent. Congratulations—you are off to a great start.

Always remember: 1. Simple is best, 2. Your baby will train you, 3. Water them and they will grow.........To be continued.

Happy parenting,
Tony Bakerink M.D.

Made in the USA
San Bernardino, CA
10 July 2015